BIEDERMEIER FURNITURE

A. Small LADY'S WRITING DESK in the style of Holl, Vienna, about 1825 to 1830
Mahogany veneer decorated with delicate inlay;
the snakes in the pedestals ebonised, the arrows gilt; bronze mounts. H. 102, W. 78, D. 49.5
From the collection of the Grand-Dukes of Baden, Schloss Schwetzingen, inv. no. G 1240
(Luthmer and Schmidt, plate 21) See p. 59

Biedermeier Furniture

GEORG HIMMELHEBER

TRANSLATED AND EDITED

by

Simon Jervis

Department of Furniture and Woodwork
Victoria and Albert Museum

FABER AND FABER · 3 QUEEN SQUARE · LONDON

First published in 1974
by Faber and Faber Limited
3 Queen Square London WC1
Printed in Great Britain
by W & J Mackay Limited, Chatham

ISBN 0 571 08719 1

Foreword

Biedermeier furniture is beginning to be appreciated in this country, although it is still far from being well understood. The upheavals of the Napoleonic wars had left the Germanic states impoverished, suffering from shortages of all kinds, and seething with unrest. In reaction to these circumstances the bourgeoisie adopted a way of life of inward-looking domesticity very different from that of the middle class in England, where victory had increased prosperity, and the grandiloquence of the Regency style was gradually being replaced by the plump and comfortable forms of the early Victorian period. Ostentation was neither sought nor easily achieved on account of general deprivation. Quiet pleasures, often of an intellectual nature, were enjoyed by a wide spectrum of the population, problems of class distinction having little importance except in the more reactionary courts. This was the age of Schubert, not of Handel.

It was against such a background that the furniture discussed in this volume was conceived. Simple in outline, ample, and without any flamboyance, it was admirably suited to the requirements of the people for whom it was made. Like the lives they led and the culture they produced, it often possessed great charm, although sometimes, surprisingly, it displayed a strikingly original use of simple geometric forms.

Naturally Biedermeier design drew much of its inspiration from the Empire style originally created to enhance the lustre of the Napoleonic court (see Serge Grandjean's monograph, *Empire Furniture*, in this series)—indeed many of the more elaborate pieces of the Biedermeier period, especially those made for the courts of Germany and Austria, may be regarded as direct off-shoots from the French stem. However, the essentially middle-class designs of Englishmen like Hepplewhite and Sheraton were also available to German cabinet-makers at the period, and German work often betrays English influence. The indigenous neo-classical forms of the eighteenth century were a further source of inspiration. But the style which developed from an amalgam of these three influences has a strong identity of its own, and fully merits the discerning treatment accorded it in the present volume.

Dr. Himmelheber is peculiarly well fitted to cover the subject, for he is at present curator of furniture at the Bayerisches Nationalmuseum in Munich, and has had wide experience in this field. He has worked with Dr. Heinrich Kreisel on the projected third volume of Kreisel's monumental *Geschichte des Deutschen Möbels*, which will cover the neo-classical period and the nineteenth century—including, of course, the Biedermeier period. The translation has been done by my colleague, Simon Jervis, who is himself a specialist in the field.

PETER THORNTON

Contents

Contents

Illustrations

13

MAP

Preface

Biedermeier furniture has been widely appreciated in Europe for two generations, which makes it remarkable that it has not so far been thought a suitable subject for a monograph. A series of important works brought recognition to the style as early as the first quarter of the century—it had formerly been considered a matter for ridicule. With the exception of a few specialized studies, however, all the authors concerned discussed Biedermeier and Empire furniture together, with the inevitable result that their estimation of Biedermeier suffered. The viewpoint they chose was ill-advised. When considered as elements of a greater whole, Empire and Biedermeier are both admittedly part of neo-classicism; but the Louis XVI style should not be left out in a wider conspectus of this kind, even if it belongs to the eighteenth century.

The significance of the term 'Biedermeier' in the history of German art has not yet been satisfactorily analysed. In painting it has been applied as a stylistic description of a specific genre corresponding to its literal meaning, which I will discuss later. In sculpture and, above all, architecture, it has been mistakenly rejected as a stylistic term. Although its meaning was established by those who ridiculed the period, just as 'Gothic' and 'Baroque', it did find acceptance and should, like those terms, be retained; today we have to remind ourselves that they too were once terms of abuse. The period from 1815 to 1830 in general, that of Biedermeier proper, does not merit the contempt lying behind the claim that there can be no such thing as Biedermeier architecture. There must be such a thing: Biedermeier, like any other style, has its own architecture. If the essential character of the style is recognized and analysed, it will become apparent that the achievements of the greatest German neo-classical architect, Karl Friedrich Schinkel, with the deepest significance for the future were pure Biedermeier.

Serge Grandjean's account of Empire furniture forms an earlier volume in this series. The Empire style, like the founder of the Empire himself, gained ground all over

Europe. It underwent local variations but, whether in Italy or in Germany, it always remained the imperial French style, having been specifically created in Paris as such. While Empire stayed a national French style, Biedermeier was, in a completely different way, a national German one. Even in France, there was a reaction to the Napoleonic style under Louis XVIII and Charles X, and, in this period, French furniture was plainer than before. The historical situation in German-speaking lands produced a more radical upheaval and with it an open and enthusiastic striving for innovation. Vienna, which was for some years the political centre of Europe, and the metropolis of an empire receptive to many different cultural influences, a city with a wealthy and cultured bourgeoisie, was in an ideal position to create a new style. The bourgeoisie created its own style both here and throughout Germany.

In Germany, the main foundations for the approaching industrial age were laid during the Biedermeier period. The chief pattern for the process was England. German attention was centred on this country which was so far ahead in economic development. Tools and machines were not the only imports from England; Germany was also influenced by English art and fashion. Contemporary English productions were studied and publicized; close attention was paid to the best English cabinet-makers, designers and decorators of the immediate past.

In this volume an attempt has been made to provide in the field of furniture the stylistic analysis for the Biedermeier period that is still lacking and to assemble, through detailed study of contemporary sources, as large as possible a corpus of facts. A number of cabinet-makers can be identified and some pieces of furniture can be attributed to particular makers. The great bulk of the furniture, however, remains anonymous. This may be regrettable but it is characteristic of the period. The style was not created by pampered court craftsmen, much sought-after as furnishers, but by a mass of unpretentious craftsmen who led a simple life—though they sometimes achieved respect and prosperity. David Roentgen, the world-famous supplier of royalty, was producing furniture almost up to the threshold of the Biedermeier period. Michael Thonet, who began as a modest Biedermeier cabinet-maker and ended as the director of a world-wide enterprise, ushered in the new, post-Biedermeier era. Roentgen and Thonet represent two different poles; the achievements of the average Biedermeier cabinet-maker fall between.

Only a small selection of their work is represented in the illustrations, which have not

18

been confined to high-quality pieces since nothing but a wide range of productions can give a true picture of a style. With one or two important exceptions the pieces are un-published, or only published in books that are difficult of access. The important illus-trated works by Folnesics, Luthmer, Lux and Schmitz will retain their value for the serious student.

My book could never have appeared in its present form without the generous assis-tance of others. First, I must thank my wife, who undertook the laborious though often entertaining task of looking through the endless contemporary accounts in the journals that were being published everywhere during the Biedermeier period. The Librarian of the Bavarian National Museum, Fräulein Edith Chorherr, gave untiring help in pro-curing these newspapers and other specialized literature. I was also given every possible assistance by the directors of museums and archives. For their invaluable advice and vigorous support, I must single out the following for thanks: Professor Arens of the University of Mainz, Professor Werner Fleischhauer of Stuttgart, Frau Carola van Ham of Cologne, Dr. Dieter-Jürgen Leister of the Bomann-Museum in Celle, Dr. Arnold Lühning of the Schleswig-Holsteinisches Landesmuseum in Schleswig, Frau Gisela Haase of the Museum für Kunsthandwerk in Dresden, the late Professor Johannes Sievers of Berlin and Dr. Gretel Wagner of the Staatliche Kunstbibliothek in Berlin.

I am especially indebted to Peter Thornton, who gave me the opportunity to write a volume in the 'Faber Monographs on Furniture' series, enthusiastically supported my choice of subject and provided me with constant assistance in my task.

GEORG HIMMELHEBER

Central Europe
in 1825

A HESSEN
B PALATINATE
C BAVARIA
D SCHLESWIG-
   HOLSTEIN
E SAXONY
F AUSTRIA
G PRUSSIA
H HANOVER
J MECKLENBURG
K THÜRINGEN
L BADEN AND
   WÜRTTEMBERG

1 Karlsbad
2 Flensburg
3 Lübeck
4 Altona
5 Hamburg
6 Oldenburg
7 Bremen
8 Celle
9 Hanover
10 Berlin
11 Potsdam
12 Posen (Pozań)
13 Brunswick
14 Düsseldorf
15 Kassel
16 Leipzig
17 Cologne
18 Weimar
19 Dresden
20 Marburg

21 Neuwied
22 Bad Homburg
23 Wiesbaden
24 Mainz
25 Darmstadt
26 Prague
27 Bamberg
28 Bayreuth
29 Mannheim
30 Fürth
31 Speyer
32 Paris
33 Nuremberg
34 Ansbach
35 Hassfurt
36 Karlsruhe
37 Eichstädt
38 Stuttgart
39 Regensburg
40 Bregenz
41 Augsburg
42 Schwetzingen
43 Freiburg
44 Vienna
45 Munich
46 Constance
47 Salzburg
48 Budapest
49 Rastatt
50 Innsbruck
51 Berne
52 Graz
53 Geneva
54 Zagreb

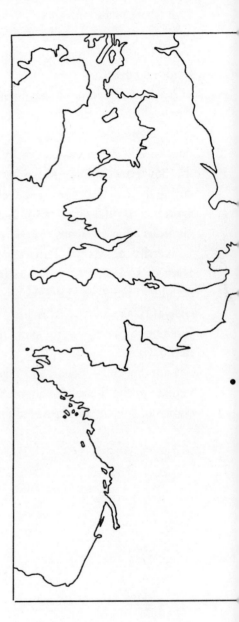

BALTIC SEA

NORTH SEA

Rhine

Rhine

Rhine

Danube

Lake
Constance

Danube

Danube

ONE

Towards a Definition of
the Biedermeier Style

THE PERIOD

The period normally called 'Biedermeier' in Germany starts with the foundation by
the Congress of Vienna in 1814–15 of the German Confederation, and ends with the
revolutions of 1848 and 1849: thirty eventful years, full of excitement, innovation and
upheaval. The newly-created middle class started ambitiously, but it was soon stifled
by the restoration of monarchy and the consequent repression.

The three allied campaigns against Napoleonic France fought mainly on German
soil, the continental blockade, and the wars of liberation left widespread poverty and
distress in Germany. Yet this very poverty seemed the source of new life. The young
men who came back from the wars of liberation had acquired new and original ideas
concerning the state and forms of government, and rightly considered themselves a
significant part of the nation. In 1815 students at Jena founded 'Burschenschaften', that
is, student organizations dedicated to the cause of German unity. The princely rulers
of Germany granted their subjects constitutions, and were generally convinced of the
rightness of such demands.

The wars of liberation brought about not only victory over enemies abroad but also
the victory of the middle classes over the privileges of the nobility. The Biedermeier
period was fundamentally middle-class. The bourgeois aspired to the education which
had hitherto been denied him and, at the universities, lectures were no longer held in
Latin but in German. Hegel and, above all, Humboldt won respect for German scholarship. Beethoven and Schubert created musical works that are now classics; Goethe's
West-Östlicher Divan, *Marienbader Elegie* and *Wilhelm Meister* were published in this
period, and the most important painters were Joseph Anton Koch, Caspar David
Friedrich and Carl Blechen. In 1816, Ludwig I of Bavaria founded the first public

museum, the Glyptothek and in 1828 Berlin, Frankfurt and Cologne followed suit. Bookshops, lending libraries and reading circles sprang up. The influence of the church was slight, and it was hoped that the two existing denominations might be united. Freedom to trade destroyed the conservative force of the guilds; the beginning of industrialization promised progress and prosperity. However, the immediate effect of both was a new insecurity and poverty among the labouring class, which was already suffering from foreign competition that inundated the German markets with imports after the long-desired lifting of the continental blockade.

Soon the German princes who had thrived in the age of absolutism began to see everything new as suspect and after the initial rapture of freedom an unparalleled reaction set in. The bureaucracy became all-powerful; steps were taken against all innovatory tendencies with the full apparatus of police, prisons and arrests. Working-class educational associations were banned, and the press, which had just begun to function in its own right for the first time, was subjected to a thoroughgoing censorship. Soon the devious forces of hypocrisy and bigotry regained their sway. The police acted against any demonstration of free thought; professors were deprived of their seats; a paralysing fear of spies and informers prevailed. This resulted, on the one hand, in the nervous middle classes leading an enclosed and cautious existence—scorned later by their descendants—and, on the other, in popular agitation coming to a peak in bloodily repressed uprisings and, finally, the revolution of 1848 and 1849. However, in the last analysis, repression and reaction were unable to retard progress and evolution, which were most clearly visible in science and technology.[1]

Within a short period, innovation was followed by reaction, and rise by decline. I will try to show that even the current style of furniture, the only subject treated here, was affected by this dichotomy. True Biedermeier is only found in the earlier 'liberal' part of the period. The beginnings of reaction can be detected in about 1830: around this date historicism and its attendant variety of styles start to become apparent—a fact which

[1] The most comprehensive work on the history of the period and its art remains Max von Boehn, *Biedermeier, Deutschland von 1815 bis 1847*, Berlin, 1911. See also the collection of contemporary sources edited by Georg Hermann, *Das Biedermeier im Spiegel seiner Zeit*, Berlin, 1913 (republished Oldenburg and Hamburg, 1965), and Günther Böhmer, *Die Welt des Biedermeier*, Munich, 1968.

has not hitherto been recognized. Therefore Biedermeier proper, the last of the neo-classical styles, can be said to have lasted only from 1815 to 1830.

THE NAME

In German 'bieder' means plain, unpretentious and inoffensive; a 'Biedermann' is an honest, upright citizen, irreproachable and solid, and without any great intellectual ambitions—or at any rate without anything approaching genius. The name 'Biedermeier' ('Meier' being one of the commonest German surnames) was invented by a doctor called Adolph Kussmaul (1822–1902), an important clinical physician and a university teacher at Heidelberg, and a friend of his called Ludwig Eichrodt (1827–1892), the chief district judge in Lahr. In 1853 Kussmaul came across the poetry of Samuel Friedrich Sauter (1766–1846), a village schoolmaster from Baden. Its unconscious humour inspired him and his friend, who was a composer of comic verse, to write ironical poems in Sauter's style under the pseudonym of 'Gottlieb Biedermaier'. 'Biedermaier' made his first appearance in Eichrodt's volume entitled *Gedichte in allerlei Humoren* in 1853 and, from 1855, appeared regularly in the humorous journal *Fliegende Blätter*.[1]

Bernward Deneke's comprehensive, thorough and informative piece of research 'Biedermeier in Mode und Kunsthandwerk 1890–1905' (1967), is the first work to have traced the genesis of the stylistic term Biedermeier.[2] Like almost all such terms it was at first intended to be derogatory. In 1886, Georg Hirth, in his big work on German furniture and interior decoration *Das Deutsche Zimmer*, categorized the period from about 1800 onwards as 'Empire-Zopf und Biedermännerei' (Empire frippery and fashions

[1] Adolph Kussmaul, *Jugenderinnerungen eines alten Arztes*, Stuttgart, 1890, p. 486ff., and A. Kennel, *Ludwig Eichrodt, ein Dichterleben*, Lahr, 1895, p. 75ff. In both publications a completely clear picture is given of the evolution of the term, 'Biedermeier', which makes it all the more remarkable that in the recent past a whole series of articles have been published presenting this evolution as a completely new discovery, and indeed somewhat confusing it. Accurate accounts are given in Rudolf Majut, 'Das literarische Biedermeier', *Germanisch-Romanische Monatsschrift*, XX, 1932, p. 401ff., and (in English) Charles A. Williams, 'Notes on the origin and history of the earlier Biedermaier', *The Journal of English and Germanic Philology*, Urbana, Illinois, LVII, 1958, p. 403ff.

[2] *Anzeiger des Germanischen Nationalmuseums*, 1967, p. 163ff.

for the Biedermann). After the Empire, he wrote, 'began that "cosy", meaningless confusion, a style in fact born of gaucherie, a style whose lack of pretension corresponded to its deficiency in true artistic qualities'.[1] 'Biedermeier' was first used in 1891 in Wilhelm Heinrich Riehl's study of the artists and craftsmen of his period; it was the usual word for the style of the 1820s and 1830s among artists of his generation.[2] In 1891, in volume five of the *Illustrierte Kunstgewerbliche Zeitschrift für Innen Dekoration*, then a very influential periodical, Georg Bötticher also spoke of 'Biedermeier' when pointing to pomposity and pedantry as the trademarks of ornament in the early nineteenth century. In the volume that followed, Fritz Minkus bemoaned the fact that, since the stylistic revivalists had taken up the Empire style again, the 'Biedermann' period might serve as a model for contemporary furniture makers: 'that pitiable "style"—if one can speak of a style whose main characteristic is its lack of style—of infinite dullness and irredeemable tastelessness, which we have long considered beneath us and held up to ridicule'. The concept of Biedermeier acquired a definite shape in Karl Rosner's book *Die dekorative Kunst im 19. Jahrhundert*, published in 1898; even so, it was defined as an unimaginative postscript to the Empire style with a rudimentary formal vocabulary, expressing the limited taste of an insipid, backward, prosaic and austere period in which ability, knowledge, taste and tradition had a limited life-span.

Thus the name of a character in a humorous magazine, expressing the very essence of an era just passed and naturally made fun of, was used by the succeeding generation as a stylistic term for the formal language of the applied art of the years between 1815 and 1830, which they totally despised.

REAPPRAISAL

The important large-scale exhibition on the theme of the Congress of Vienna put on by the Österreichisches Museum für Kunst und Industrie in 1896 marks the beginning of a new and more objective attitude towards Biedermeier. The foreword of the catalogue described it as 'a period rich in brilliant and significant achievements, a period of vigour

---

[1] 3rd ed., Hirth, 1886, p. 46.

[2] *Der moderne Benvenuto Cellini, Kulturgeschichtliche Charakterköpfe*, Stuttgart, 1891, p. 170.

and creativity in the history of both Austria and Vienna, to which we all have reason to look back with pride'. Admittedly it was Empire furniture that was singled out for praise and recommended as an example for contemporary makers to follow. Nor was there any lack of critics who saw in Biedermeier nothing but a middle-class version of Empire, and spoke of a 'Bureau' or 'Kanzlei' style. However, the fact that the period was now felt to be a worthy subject for an exhibition soon had results. The exhibition was a great success at all levels and, at the same time, a starting-point for scholarly research into the period. Even the exhibitions of contemporary applied art held in the same year in Dresden and Berlin, showed clear indications of currents of influence emanating from the Congress of Vienna exhibition. As early as 1898 the architects Hellwig and Haiger designed a décor in the Biedermeier style for the art exhibition in the Glaspalast in Munich. At the winter exhibition of the Österreichisches Museum in the same year the quality of Biedermeier—a 'real Vienna style'—was again praised as an ideal; Hartwig Fischel referred repeatedly to its significance for the modern style.[1] So also did Joseph Hoffmann, one of the great figures of Viennese art nouveau, who recognized his own debt to Biedermeier.

The first art-historical treatises on the Biedermeier style were also published in Vienna. Joseph Folnesics' work *Innenräume und Hausrat der Empire- und Biedermeierzeit in Österreich-Ungarn*, still an indispensable collection of illustrations, though without any explanatory text, first appeared in 1902 and had gone through five editions by 1922. Also in 1902, A. Schestag began to publish the results of his researches in an article in the Viennese journal, *Kunst und Kunsthandwerk*, entitled 'Zur Entstehung und Entwicklung des Biedermeierstils'. In this first scholarly analysis of the style, it was already clearly recognized that although Biedermeier developed from the Empire style, often closely resembling it in its forms, it was completely different in character and foreign in essence to the Empire style. Developing an insight expressed by Peter Jessen in 1893, Schestag stated that after the Empire style, which was of French origin, Germany looked back to the formal language of late eighteenth-century English furniture.[2]

In 1904 Ferdinand Luthmer's work *Bürgerliche Möbel aus dem ersten Drittel des 19.*

[1] 'Das Interieur', *Wiener Monatsheft für angewandte Kunst*, I, 1900, p. 97; and II, 1901, p. 65.
[2] Peter Jessen, 'Der kunstgewerbliche Geschmack in England', *Kunstgewerbeblatt*, new series, IV, 1893, p. 67.

Jahrhunderts appeared, and in 1906 Josef August Lux's picture-book *Von der Empire—zur Biedermeierzeit* followed. Like Paul Mebes in his volume called *Um 1800, Architektur und Handwork im letzten Jahrhundert ihrer traditionellen Entwicklung*, which came out two years later, Lux presented works of the Biedermeier period as models for contemporary craftsmen. Once again the style of the immediate past—in this case art nouveau—is rejected, but there was also dissatisfaction with the limitations of a style that did not answer the needs of the present (a dissatisfaction also apparent in art nouveau itself), which resulted in a hankering after the simple forms of the pre-industrial era. Lux expressly named Biedermeier furniture as the prototype of the modern furniture of his time. It is interesting to note that even a basically reactionary manufacturer of 'period furniture', the Erfurt firm of Ziegenhorn and Jucker, came down completely on the side of Biedermeier as opposed to art nouveau in a polemical pamphlet published in 1908.[1]

Thus, within the space of a few years, there had been a complete reappraisal of the Biedermeier style; what had been scornfully rejected was now enthusiastically recommended.

Further reaction in favour of the Biedermeier style after the First World War was understandable. The essential affinity of this period of deprivation—accompanied by a break-through in the search for a long-desired freedom—to that which followed the wars of liberation was evident. The years 1919 to 1923 saw the appearance of the important volumes on Biedermeier furniture by Hartwig Fischel, a Viennese art-nouveau architect, Hermann Schmitz, Ferdinand Luthmer and Robert Schmidt. The revival of Biedermeier, which was not confined to the worst architects of the period, was the basis for the ultimate development of the pure and completely unpretentious style of the Bauhaus, noble in its simplicity.

THE LIMITS OF THE PERIOD

The commencement of the Biedermeier style coincided with a political revolution, indeed, it was an element in that revolution. The end of the Napoleonic era, which had

[1] *Rückblick auf die historischen Möbelformen im Zusammenhang mit der modernen Raumkunst*, Erfurt, 1908.

been so much longed for, also marked the end of the Napoleonic style, Empire. Its formalized character was felt to be 'cold'; it was too pretentious for a period full of poverty and distress, and too imperial for a period full of liberal ideas. Nor, when the last German princes had deserted Napoleon after the battle of Leipzig, did Empire have any hold in the courts of Germany. In every sphere England was now the important influence. Thus arose a new variation of the neo-classicism which had started with the Louis XVI style of the last quarter of the eighteenth century.

The Biedermeier furniture style remained a neo-classical style. Like Louis XVI and Empire, its formal repertoire was ultimately supplied by antiquity. Furniture had flat surfaces; it was built up from geometrical forms; and column and pediment, mouldings and beading, were its predominant decorative elements.

The period generally described as Biedermeier in the history of art and civilization also ended with a violent political event, the revolution of 1848 and 1849. However, contrary to general opinion, the neo-classical furniture style of the Biedermeier period had already come to an end almost two decades earlier, around the year 1830.

The surviving furniture of the years 1830 to 1850 has not yet been classified. I say 'surviving' since in the second half of the century immense technical progress, increased prosperity, arrogance and ignorance resulted in a shocking destruction of most of what had lasted till then. For this reason documentary sources provide the only guide to artistic currents in cabinet-making. On the other hand, these—in the form of reports on exhibitions and pattern-books—were published in greater numbers than ever before.

The first German exhibition of art and industry took place at Stuttgart in 1812; its sponsor, King Friedrich I of Württemberg, was following French ideas, for, in Paris, similar shows of models for industry had been held regularly in the Louvre from 1798 onwards. In 1815 Munich followed, in 1816 Düsseldorf and Leipzig, and soon no year passed without there being one or more exhibitions of industry, most of them including a presentation of medals or prizes. More or less complete descriptions of the furniture exhibited can be culled from the official reports.

The romantic movement of the late eighteenth century had already produced a revival of the Gothic style. This taste never completely died out, and the style was sporadically fashionable during the Biedermeier period—at least in individual motifs. In 1813, 1816 and from 1825 to 1829, furniture incorporating Gothic elements was repeatedly shown at exhibitions. But the year 1830 witnessed a whole range of stylistic revivals. While Gothic furniture was becoming ever commoner, furniture in a revived Baroque style made its appearance for the first time in this year. The report on the 1830 Berne Exhibition said of the cabinet-maker, Stehlin of Geneva, that 'his tables would, perhaps, have been more admired at the court of Louis XIV than by our generation'.[1] The report on cabinet-making at the 1834 Munich Exhibition described the situation thus: 'One can now see pieces in the most varied styles, from Chinese to Greek, reflecting the full variety of contemporary thought.'[2] Nevertheless, furniture in the Gothic style predominated, and the same thing happened the next year, when the most notable pieces were those designed for Schloss Hohenschwangau, the Gothic castle which was under construction for the Crown Prince of Bavaria of the day, later King Max II. It happened again at Hanover in 1837 and at Düsseldorf in 1838, when the cabinet-maker Carl Hilgers exhibited 'a ladies' work-table, in a free Gothic style, in palisander wood with copper inlay'. This shows a mixture of Gothic with Boulle work, which had already, at the 1835 Munich Exhibition, been said to have become 'naturalized'. In 1839 Renaissance and Rococo suddenly appeared by the side of Gothic and Baroque, and so the indiscriminate use of all historical styles alongside one another—the distinguishing feature of historicism—was finally established.

A similar picture emerges from the pattern-books of the period, although these were, as so often happens, only in the rarest instances really creative or even avant-garde. Architects, such as Carl Heideloff (b. Stuttgart, 1789; d. Hassfurt, 1865), whose work *Der Bau- und Möbelschreiner oder Ebenist* was published in several instalments between 1832 and 1837, had great influence. Most of his designs were in the Gothic style. Gothic forms also crop up in sofas, secretaires and tables illustrated in the pattern-books of Marius Wölfer and Friedrich Wilhelm Mercker, which were published at Leipzig from 1830 onwards.[3] At the end of the 1830s the Rococo style made its appearance, although it was first traceable in the *Journal für Möbelschreiner und Tapezierer*, which was published

---

[1] Karl Brunner, *Bericht über die im Julius 1830 in Bern eröffnete Industrie-Ausstellung*, Bern, 1830, p. 57.

[2] *Bericht der königl. Bayerischen Ministerial-Commission über die 1834 in München stattgehabte Industrie-Ausstellung*, Munich, 2nd ed., 1836, p. 129.

[3] Marius Wölfer, *Modell- und Musterbuch für Bau- und Möbel-Tischler*, Quedlinburg and Leipzig, 1833; Friedrich Wilhelm Mercker, *Practische Zeichnungen von Meubles*, Leipzig, 1831–36.

from 1835 onwards by the Mainz cabinet-maker and drawing-master, Wilhelm Kimbel, and enjoyed an enormous circulation. In the early 1840s the whole range of stylistic revivals—Gothic, Renaissance, Baroque and Rococo—was represented in this journal.

Another interesting point is that in the 1830s there was a remarkable increase in the numbers of these pattern-books; they were needed far more in this period of stylistic revivals than in that of the Biedermeier style. A cabinet-worker's workshop during the Biedermeier period differed little from a carpenter's shop in the later Middle Ages. The craftsman was familiar with the forms he used; this middle-class master had created them himself for his middle-class customers. In contrast to the Empire period, and indeed to the Baroque and Rococo periods, scarcely any designs for furniture were provided by artists. In fact, design was part of the apprenticeship of the cabinet-maker, and his master-piece still had to be executed from his own design. The master of the guild, who conducted the examination, scrutinized the design as well as its execution. Naturally, even at this period cabinet-makers went to a variety of sources for inspiration. Moreover, pattern-books, in which architects had laid down the correct style for furniture, had also been available during the preceding Empire period; significantly, all these were closely dependent on Percier and Fontaine's *Recueil* both in their style of draughtsmanship and their printing. In the whole period from 1815 to 1830, however, the total of pattern-books published scarcely exceeded that in any single year of the 1830s! By then the current style was no longer that created by the cabinet-maker, but one which presupposed knowledge of earlier periods.

Much the same holds true of the technical journals, which were published for the most part by the recently founded trade associations, and of the literary and fine-arts journals, which were also a regular source of design for the decorative arts. Many of these latter, most notably Bertuch's *Journal des Luxus und der Moden*, had been in circulation since the eighteenth century, and in the first two decades of the nineteenth century one or two new titles appeared each year. In this field too, however, there was a rapid increase, starting in 1833; after that date five or more new titles a year were by no means uncommon.

The ultimate cause of the ending of the Biedermeier style was the approach of the industrial age. Machines had, admittedly, already aroused great interest earlier in the nineteenth century; not a year had passed without accounts of new wood-working machines appearing in the trade journals. The most important innovation had been the introduction of the circular saw, which had been brought back from England in 1818 by Stöber, a Munich entrepreneur. However, these were isolated experiments that had had no effect on workshops in general. But in the 1830s and, above all, the 1840s a different situation developed: there was a rapid increase in the literature on machinery, and machines began to gain a progressively stronger foothold in workshops, which were gradually increasing in size. Hand in hand with the process went a definite tendency towards specialization among workers and their functions. In 1822, and again in 1828, admiring accounts of Roguin's fully mechanized factory at Port de la Gare, near Paris, appeared in the trade journals. It was stated that this establishment, where a steam-engine drove all the machines for sawing, planing, rabbeting and splitting, was the beginning of a revolution among cabinet-makers.[1] In 1831 Stutzer, a Berlin pattern-maker, exhibited a machine 'for cutting wood in a curve', in other words a band-saw—a tool for which Ferdinand Selle, a cabinet-maker from Potsdam, was awarded a patent in 1836.[2] In the same year Wenzel Sandner of Schlaurakonitz in Bohemia installed a steam-driven saw-mill, and the brothers Pallenberg converted to steam a veneer-cutting machine they had installed some time before in their furniture factory at Cologne.[3] The industrial age was beginning to influence German furniture workshops.

As a style in the decorative arts and especially in furniture, therefore, Biedermeier lasted only for the fifteen-year period from 1815 to 1830—its formal repertoire will be discussed in the following chapter. However, no artistic style suddenly ends in a given year and in the 1830s there were of course stragglers who continued to work in the Biedermeier idiom. But the path of the future was already signposted and historicism, as a part of the romantic movement, had already begun.

[1] *Jahrbücher des k.k. polytechnischen Instituts in Wien*, V, 1824, p. 384ff.; and *Königl. priv. Schleswig-Holstein-Lauenburgischer Gewerbsfreund*, I, 1829, col. 420.

[2] *Verhandlungen des Vereins zur Beförderung des Gewerbefleisses in Preussen*, X, 1831, p. 172; and XVI, 1837, p. 106.

[3] *Mitteilungen für Gewerbe und Handel* (Böhmen), II, 1836, p. 217; and *Wöchentl. Beiblatt zum Allg. Organ des Gewerb-Vereins zu Köln*, XLIV, 1836.

I. SECRETAIRE, Berlin, 1811
Designer, KARL FRIEDRICH SCHINKEL. Maker, BERNHARD WANSCHAFF
Veneered with burr birch, decorated with reliefs and mounts of cast-iron
Schloss Montbijou, Berlin (Sievers, plate 173 (see Bibliography, p. 105)) See p. 47

II. Secretaire, Vienna, about 1810
Veneered with mahogany, decorated with gilt carving, and bronze mounts by FRANZ DETTLER. H. 160, W. 100, D. 45
Österreichisches Museum für angewandte Kunst, Vienna, inv. no. H2027 (Meister and Jedding, plate 523)
See pp. 48, 61 and 84

TWO

The Formal Vocabulary of
the Biedermeier Style

THE BASIC ELEMENTS

Biedermeier was a style created by the middle class for the middle class. Furniture designs were not supplied by architects, as had been the case with the Empire style which preceded it, but by the craftsmen themselves. The outlook of the craftsman with all its advantages and drawbacks was, in consequence, one of the most important constituent elements of the Biedermeier style. The imagination of the craftsman and the realities of craftsmanship governed the development of its forms. This implied the 'truth to materials' which was preached throughout the whole of the late nineteenth century and during the art nouveau period, and which was, to a large extent, achieved by the Bauhaus. Absolute 'truth to materials' is unattainable, and not really worth striving for. Nevertheless, neither before nor in the period of historicism which followed was a style's development from its raw material as important a factor as it was during the Biedermeier period. Doing justice to the materials was the overriding principle. Wood was the basic material, and the plank the basis of construction. Wood was prized to an unprecedented degree, and became the fundamental form of decoration in Biedermeier furniture. The plank became the dominant formal element: glued into large sheets (and, of course, veneered) it formed smooth, level surfaces. Having lost their load-bearing function, vertical mouldings and pilasters ceased to have any architectural or sculptural function and became merely flat applied strips. Base, cornice and pediment were, in most cases, reduced to the simple plank. By such means the style's basis in craftsmanship was intentionally made visible. For example, the joints of seat rails and legs, and the joined construction of *étagères*, were openly revealed.

Raw materials and tools, therefore, were determining factors in the creation of the Biedermeier style, which was also vitally affected by the attitudes of the middle-class

33

craftsman—a factor that aroused the scorn and contempt of the succeeding generation of 'decorative artists'.

But its materials were not the only point of departure in the formal development of the style: the purpose of the furniture—its function—also played a part. Functionalism—the adjustment of furniture to its purpose—was not admittedly a discovery of the Biedermeier period; the way furniture is made has always been intimately related to its function. But its required functions have undergone continual changes. The purpose of every chair is to be sat upon, yet in the Baroque and Rococo periods the very act of sitting took different forms, and the same is true of the Empire period. The Empire style's pretentiousness resulted in people behaving in an ostentatious manner. In every period before Biedermeier the importance of furniture—peasant furniture excluded—as a means of ostentation, or of displaying personal status, had outweighed its function in the home. The 'Biedermann' wanted to combine sitting comfortably and maintaining his dignity; he wanted to feel at home.

Before the Empire period every individual piece of furniture had had its permanent and immutable position in the ensemble of a room. It was a part of the architecture, and a background for the people who moved about in front of it. A Rococo console table's function consisted in its position against a wall into which, thanks to the decoration of the panelling or plasterwork, it almost merged. Biedermeier furniture, on the other hand, was, for the first time, really movable. It stood in the body of the room ready to be shifted about; people lived around it, instead of in front of it.

The Biedermeier table, which was usually round, was not positioned formally in the centre of the room, but 'cosily' in a corner. It was used for meals, and also for sitting round in comfort, for conversation, needlework and reading. The secretaire of the period stood against the wall and was used for writing on, but in it could also be locked up all the letters, diaries, and books of verses that played such a large part in the life of the age. There was no regimentation in it, as there had been on the bureau plat of the eighteenth century. Which corner the table was to occupy, and which wall the secretaire should stand against, were considered unimportant questions. Pieces of furniture were interchangeable and room arrangements could be changed at will.

Truth to materials and functionalism were the basic principles in the evolution of the Biedermeier style and its forms. The resultant use of the plank produced the surface flatness that is a pervading characteristic of the style. This flatness led to the stressing of a single viewpoint. Biedermeier chest furniture had a distinct display side; it was neither conceived three-dimensionally nor intended to be walked round. Even seat furniture was executed with a totally frontal viewpoint; it lacked a profile. Flatness affected every aspect of furniture, even methods of decoration. In fact this tendency towards flatness even outweighed the concept of honest craftsmanship, normally the dominant principle, thus providing evidence for the proposition that the interior dynamic of a style is always ultimately more powerful than any striving for truth to materials. From the craftsman's point of view the right method of achieving a flat surface is to divide it into load-bearing framework and panels variable within that framework. However, Biedermeier furniture shunned this framework-panel method of construction. If the flat surface was articulated, this was achieved with shallow sunk panels which avoided the impression of a framework; they were usually rhomboid, semi-circular, elongated semi-circles or segment-shaped. If they were rectangular or square, the resultant frame was minimized by carrying the veneer over frame and sunk panel alike; the grain, therefore, ran vertically over horizontal friezes.

Methods of decoration were subordinated to this love of surface flatness. For example, neither colonnades nor caryatids nor even horizontal mouldings were allowed to interrupt it; they were never sculptural decoration but instead formed another layer of flatness, a slight nuance, a thin second stratum. Carved decoration, commonest on sofas, penetrated the flat wood but never converted it into three-dimensional ornament. Glass-fronted cabinets mostly had rather wide divisions between their panes, which helped to close up the visual hiatus in the flat surface caused by the pane of glass; they gave an indication of where the flat surface should be, as did the rails in the backs of benches and chairs. Here again the tendency of the style towards flatness was more powerful than any striving towards truth to materials. The fact that these rails, these samples of flatness, are constructed of several pieces of wood joined together is, as far as possible, concealed. In fact they looked as if they had been sawn out of a single flat piece.

Every piece of furniture, even a Biedermeier piece, must of necessity be three-dimensional. Different planes meet in it and produce distinct, rectilinear cubes. The Biedermeier piece of furniture, however, never consisted of a single unified cube; it was built up of separate cubes placed next to one another or inside one another on the same level. The square feet of a piece of chest furniture abutted on the cube formed by its base. The top drawer of a commode often jutted out from its flat front as a separate cube. The top sections of furniture were also made up of separate cubes, often arranged as steps. The pediments that surmounted pieces of furniture, were applied like flat planks to the basic cube, or merely distinguished from the flat front surface of the cube by a small applied moulding. In this way, the typical piece of Biedermeier furniture acquired a composite character, which is further evidence of its basis in craftsmanship, and of its close relation to its function.

Empire furniture, on the other hand, was based upon an architectural system. It looked as if it had been built and could have been executed in marble or granite. Rococo furniture, at its most perfect, looked like a sculptural creation; flatness and right angles were, as far as possible, excluded. It could be cast as a unit from bronze, and so formed in plastic materials (in the Louis XVI period wax models were still made for furniture—a notion which would have seemed absurd during the Biedermeier period.)[1] Biedermeier furniture too included some curved shapes, although these were curved planes or rails rather than swellings of the Rococo type. The planes were always concavely curved but never *bombé*. Even completely circular pieces of furniture or parts of furniture avoided giving the impression of swelling shapes but appeared as vestigial or, more often, trimmed cubes. The circle achieved its effect within the plane.

Just as cubes were attached to one another, so also could curved shapes be placed on cubes, in which case they were usually linked to one another by concave incurved connecting sections. Concave curved planes of this type were also sometimes used as basic shapes; for example, in bases and cornices.

The Biedermeier penchant for pure geometrical forms even resulted in furniture which included spherical sections: in particular work-tables, waste-paper baskets, and the like. They displayed the cabinet-maker's skill as a craftsman; indeed, the ultimate reason for their creation was to show off this skill. The degree of virtuosity involved in the execution of such a piece of furniture where, for instance, one half of a sphere might be made to fit into the other, was almost equal to that of a violin-maker.

Rails were curved in exactly the same way as plane surfaces. After the plank, the rail

---

[1] Adolf Feulner, *Kunstgeschichte des Möbels*, Berlin, 3rd ed., 1930, p. 668; Juliette Niclausse, 'The Jewel-Cabinet of the Dauphine Marie-Antoinette', *Journal of the Walters Art Gallery*, XVIII, 1955, p. 69.

or squared timber is the most obvious constructional element in furniture. Biedermeier chair- and table-legs had, as their basis, the squared timber, but never appeared curved, like a Rococo leg; instead they seemed bent. The curve was precise and abrupt, and there was always something tense and resilient about it. It is significant, therefore, that in work-tables, for example, a basket-like construction assembled from individual rails, which were apparently bent, was favoured. The stretchers of small tables were also often curved upwards in the centre, where they supported a small tray or a vase.

Bent plane surfaces frequently formed the top rails of chairs, representing a coincidence between stylistic and functional considerations. A top rail which was bent forwards at the sides made leaning back comfortable; the sitter felt protected and at home. Curved surfaces, which were not really bent, also afforded a demonstration of technical virtuosity.

The desire for domesticity had an effect on the size of furniture. Biedermeier furniture scarcely ever exceeded the human scale; the upper limit of chest furniture was usually at eye level or a little above it; even wardrobes were often remarkably low.

The primary and most important decorative element in Biedermeier furniture was the wood itself, as I have said. The visible structure of wood, its grain, was exploited to the maximum effect. Cabinet-makers were always at pains to make use of the qualities of their woods, the different colours and varied textures. Previously these effects had been used to articulate or subdivide flat surfaces, to contrast with other means of decoration, to create pictorial effects, as in the case of marquetry, or to imitate a completely different material such as marble or stonework. Biedermeier furniture eschewed such tricks. Instead, the Biedermeier craftsman thought in terms of the material he knew. The veneer used on a piece of furniture, however large, always came from a single tree. It was joined vertically, and generally abutted in a central seam, but in any case so as to produce a single unbroken length that expressed the upward growth of the tree. Thus the basic material, the plank, once again produced a formal solution based on the plane surface.

In contrast to undecorated wood, marquetry became much less important, although it did not, it is true, entirely die out. Nonetheless marquetry never completely covered the surface of a piece of Biedermeier furniture. Motifs inlaid in a circular or oval format, including the favourite scallop, a shell or a flower, were used. Rays and star shapes also occurred, as did tendrils covering broad areas, stringing lines and framing bands, which stressed the shape of the individual cube but never outlined the complete piece of furniture. Sunken panels were sometimes veneered with differently coloured or grained woods.

In ambitious pieces of furniture, successful use was sometimes made of framed pictures in other materials such as painted porcelain plaques, or engravings under glass. Sunken panels or pediments were sometimes decorated with paintings executed directly on the wood and inspired, for the most part, by vase paintings.

The whole repertoire of classicism, with which cabinet-makers had been conversant since the Louis XVI period, also remained available as a source of decorative motifs.

As before, columns were very popular; but it was only in the rarest instances that they extended to the full height of a piece of furniture. They were usually confined to recesses in the basic cube of the piece, and thus exchanged their load-bearing function for the purely decorative purpose of articulating the flat plane. In the interiors of secretaires they were often used in quantity, producing the effect of a railing, and looked as if they could be slid along the line. Their bases and capitals were no longer made of solid bronze but were usually executed in the same wood as the columns. The columns themselves were frequently ebonized, but occasionally made of alabaster.

Herms and caryatids were a legacy of the Empire style; they mostly had heads of an Egyptian cast, often combined with naturalistically modelled human feet. Lion paws were another popular form of decoration; they often provided the feet of cupboards and most often, tables, although they were rarely very naturalistically modelled. On curved table-legs, for instance, the paw represented a mere extension of the leg rather than an emphasis of the foot.

Sphinxes, dolphins and, above all, swans were popular as decorative motifs, particularly on sofas and beds, despite their frequently comical aspect. The acanthus retained its importance, as did leaf mouldings and reed garlands in every possible variation, derivative and distortion. Vases came into fashion again, and bead and cyma mouldings were as popular as ever. The lyre, another motif from the Empire repertoire, although not encountered then with nearly the same frequency or in so many varied positions as in the Biedermeier period, was in fashion everywhere: it was used not only as a small-scale decorative motif, but also to form the side supports of small tables. Eventually, it came to determine the form of whole pieces of furniture, in which its shape may be sometimes so transformed as to be scarcely recognizable.

MATERIALS AND TECHNIQUES

In the Empire period mahogany was the only type of wood used for furniture worthy of mention. Its smooth, virtually invisible grain was in effect intended to make people forget that it really was a wood, and its dense texture made it specially well suited to polishing. Both these qualities were necessary requirements for Empire furniture.

In the Biedermeier period the use of mahogany died out almost entirely. Economic reasons were, of course, partly responsible for the reversion of craftsmen to native woods, but more important was the conscious rejection of the Empire style of the courts, a rejection that naturally had an effect on the materials used. Craftsmen favoured lighter woods, which were more in tune with the striving for comfort. The desire to use the grain as a means of decoration resulted in a search for more vividly grained woods. In the 1820s, however, mahogany again came into fashion, both in the North, and in the South. However, it was most widely used in North Germany, mainly because of the close relations with England. But because it continued to be an expensive imported commodity, there were numerous attempts to imitate it, dating back to the Empire period. Throughout the first half of the nineteenth century, in fact, trade journals and manuals were continually publishing tips and recipes on how to make home-grown woods look like mahogany.

Walnut was the wood most suited to the decorative requirements of the Biedermeier period; its attractive grain and considerable variety of colour made it suitable for a wide range of applications. It was never stained.

Bright light colours were preferred, in the same way that simple geometric forms were favoured. These requirements were best met by fruit-woods, especially as these also had a warm tone which corresponded to the Biedermeier desire for comfort. It is for this reason that maple-wood, for instance, which, although even lighter, is cooler in tone, was very rarely used, except sometimes for contrasting inlays. On the other hand, pear-wood and, in particular, cherry wood were the favourite woods after walnut. Compared to these all other woods paled into insignificance, though ash, elm and, occasionally, poplar were also used. Oak, which had been so popular until well into the Louis XVI period, especially in North Germany and the Rhineland, was never employed.

The quintessential piece of Biedermeier furniture could completely dispense with decoration and mounts. Admittedly such pieces were only made in the rarest instances; there were always drawer handles and keyhole escutcheons suitable for execution in metal. The bronze mount, therefore, remained a feature of Biedermeier furniture, even if it was nearly always replaced by a mount of thin brass sheet stamped out on a pattern. Here again the motifs were for the most part drawn from the Empire repertoire. They included griffins, genii, lions' masks, sun-chariots, herms, lotuses and rosettes; alongside these, however, were used motifs evolved by the Biedermeier style itself, which recalled the Louis XVI period—swags of drapery, vases, bunches of flowers, cornucopiae and the like.

As well as these mounts stamped from sheet metal, there were imitations made of moulded plaster which were gilded or bronzed, and thus preserved the outward appearance of bronze mounts. Purely ornamental mounts, the heads of caryatids, lions' masks as finials or as capitals and lions'-paw feet were generally executed in plaster in this way. In 1816 papier-mâché, a recently rediscovered decorative material, was introduced into Germany from France.

At about the same time the retired principal model designer of the Berlin porcelain factory, Menke, discovered a method of manufacturing, from mahogany sawdust and various other ingredients, a soft adaptable material, which went as hard as stone when exposed to the air. He founded a factory, in which he produced candelabra, chandeliers, containers, picture frames, whole statues and, above all, embellishments for furniture, in this material. Schinkel gave the firm considerable help by using embellishments of this type on the furniture he designed for the court. The trade journals contained reports of an invention by Peter Hamelin, an Englishman who, in 1817, obtained a patent on the manufacture of a cement-like material, suitable for making ornaments, from river sand, portland stone and other ingredients.[1] From the 1820s onwards reports on, and recipes for such 'Massen' (stuffs) or 'Pasten' (pastes), also called 'Steinpappe' (stone-pulp) or 'Holzbronze' (wood-bronze), were continually and repeatedly published in the trade journals. They were almost always composed of sawdust, although sometimes waste

---

[1] *Wöchentlicher Anzeiger für Kunst und Gewerbe-Fleiss im Königreich Bayern*, 1816, col. 425; 1817, col. 454; and 1818, col. 617.

paper was used, combined with an enormous variety of binding agents—size, tragacanth, rosin, wax, shellac, gum arabic, etc.

In the Biedermeier period the technique of furniture construction differed little from that of earlier periods. Improvements in tools and new machines will be described later. However, they did not have a crucial influence on the traditional methods of the cabinet-maker, which had undergone little fundamental change since the end of the Gothic era.

Large, flat surfaces without subdivisions were the only source of new problems. As in the Baroque and Rococo periods, these were usually executed in a frame and panel system of construction, whereby the panels were securely fixed in the same plane as their frames with glue. This system certainly helped to prevent warping, but it did not eliminate the possibility of splitting. In 1827 news was published in Germany of the invention by Samuel Pratt, an Englishman, of a method of reinforcing wood with iron[1] and, in fact, table tops into which flat iron strips have been fitted are known. They made the wood completely stable, without preventing its essential expansion and shrinkage.

The insertion of the bottom of the drawer in a groove from behind had long been standard practice in England and France but, with some isolated exceptions, it was an innovation only generally adopted in Germany during the Biedermeier period. Cabinet-makers and technicians as distinguished as the two Roentgens had devoted considerable thought to the problem of achieving a perfectly smooth drawer action, and had also used the countersunk drawer bottom, which allows the drawer to run on its sides alone. Nevertheless, this method did not become fully established until the Biedermeier period.

In 1826 Joseph Schwab, a Viennese cabinet-maker's journeyman obtained a patent for his invention of a method of 'manufacturing drawers in such a way that they never become stuck, and, even when they are very heavily loaded, can easily be opened and shut.'[2] This must have referred to a method of construction similar to that illustrated by Sheraton in a universal table shown in Plate 25 of his *Cabinet-Maker and Upholsterer's Drawing-Book*.

The pivot hinge was almost invariably used for doors and fall-fronts; as it was

---

[1] *Jahrbücher des k.k. polytechnischen Instituts in Wien*, X, 1827, p. 182.

[2] Stephan Ritter von Keess and W. C. W. Blumenbach, *Systematische Darstellung der neuesten Fortschritte in den Gewerben und Manufacturen*, Vienna, 1829, p. 747.

completely invisible, it fulfilled the Biedermeier cabinet-maker's desire to interrupt the flat surface as little as possible, and to expose the minimum amount of metal.

FURNITURE TYPES

The secretaire was not an invention of the Biedermeier style. It had already been very popular in the eighteenth century, and was actually the prescribed masterpiece in the majority of guilds; ultimately its form was derived from the Renaissance writing cabinet. However, there is no doubt that it was especially popular during the Biedermeier period, as it satisfied all the predilections of the age. It was economical in space; if it was not being used for writing, the fall-front could be raised and shut. It was versatile, simultaneously a writing-desk and a cupboard. It could accommodate an infinity of little drawers, lockers and secret compartments, which were so important for all the little treasures and secrets, all the modest collectors' items, albums and mementos that played such a vital part in middle-class life of the period.

Its arrangement was nearly always the same: it had three drawers or, sometimes, two doors, in its lower section; its central section was filled by the large fall-front, behind which the cabinet-maker was able to give free rein to his imagination and delight in decoration, by dividing up the interior into pigeon-holes and drawers. This, comprising the basic piece of furniture, was often surmounted by a narrower additional section, which either contained another compartment with a door, or embodied a second fall-front that served for writing in the standing position.

During the Biedermeier period great popularity was enjoyed by the so-called 'Patent-sekretär', a small, light piece of furniture looking like a fire-screen. It was almost entirely composed of the fall-front fitted in a frame, its narrow width only affording room for a few slender drawers. In about 1815 Adolph Friedrich Voigt, a Berlin cabinet-maker, produced an exceptionally fine example (Plates 86 and 87), which was also extremely significant for the sources of the Biedermeier style, as will be shown. A sketch for a patent secretaire of the type by Karl Friedrich Schinkel also survives.[1] In France heavy Empire versions of this kind of furniture were produced, with the title '*écran*

[1] Johann Sievers, *Die Möbel, Karl Friedrich Schinkel Lebenswerk*, Berlin, 1950, plate 162.

pupitre.[1] It was a type uniquely suited to match the requirements of the Biedermeier period: small, light and very versatile, with a shape resulting from a revealed and simple system of construction.

The commode remained popular, and was joined by the pier commode, or *chiffonière*; a practical piece for storing linen, this heightened commode was another product of the Biedermeier liking for everything useful. It combined an economical use of space with perfect accessibility. Although it too was not a Biedermeier invention (it followed a French Louis XVI prototype), it became, nonetheless, a piece of furniture typical of the period.

The table played a greater part in the Biedermeier period than ever before. The new style of living in the family circle that created separate islands[2] of activity in the room, had the effect of directing the craftsman's attention to this piece of furniture in particular. No living-room was without its large, round table; its top, with a deep apron into which drawers could be introduced, was generally supported on a robust central column of baluster form, itself standing on vigorously curved volutes, a tripod, or on four characteristic feet, which curved strongly outwards. But here again this curve did not produce a really dynamic shape; it had more the effect of a springy yielding of the leg beneath the weight of the table. Looking back today, it seems a natural next step that these springy feet should have been given the form of dolphins.

As well as the round table there was the rectangular 'sofa table', which could often be extended by means of flaps on each side, and could thus serve as a dining-table. It usually had four curved legs, frequently with stretchers or a stretcher shelf. In addition there was an infinite variety, ranging from small to miniature, of work-tables, designed for women's pastimes, with numerous little drawers and pigeon-holes, draw-leaves, fitted needle-cushions and little bowls for colours. They were the most ingenious and original Biedermeier forms, displaying the infinite powers of invention of the cabinet-makers who created them.

However, they were also a document of the new status of the middle-class housewife in the Biedermeier period. The social duties and amusements which, since time immemorial, had been imposed upon the fair sex at court, were foreign to her, but she was

---

[1] Sotheby's Sale, Villa Demidoff, Pratolino, 21–24 iv 1969, lot 245.
[2] Friederike Klauner, *Der Wohnraum im Wiener Biedermeier*, Vienna, 1941 (MS doctoral thesis).

also excluded from scholarship and the professions. She was, therefore, in a position to devote most of her time to feminine accomplishments, and to handiwork in all its forms and varieties. The most attractive testimony of this industry has come down to us in the form of embroidery in every technique, on material, canvas or paper, and exquisite paintings and leaves from albums.

The console table was not a Biedermeier type of furniture, as it required a fixed position in the room, which ran counter to the flexible conception of furnishing held at this period. However, in a few grand houses it was still used, and, in these cases, its form was strongly indebted to Empire prototypes.

The vitrine was another typical Biedermeier piece that was not an invention of the period; a glazed cupboard for the display of collections had already been produced in the eighteenth century. But now no middle-class living-room was without one; in it the 'treasures', the numerous souvenirs of this romantic and sentimental period, were displayed with petit-bourgeois pride—the loving-cups drunk to pledge friendship, finger-bowls, collectors' cups, christening presents, any personal possessions, all safely locked up and protected from the dust. Similar functions were fulfilled by *étagères*, elegant open racks onto which one could also put books and music, or by dumb-waiters that provided surfaces on which to rest things at tea or coffee time. All these pieces were made in such a way that their system of construction was clearly revealed; usually they consisted of a joined framework, into which doors and panes of glass were fitted.

Vitrines and small cupboards were often arranged as corner furniture, in which case their fronts were generally curved in a segment. With limited living space, such pieces cleverly made full use of the corners of a room; but they were created primarily for aesthetic reasons, their shape resulting from the desire to make the corners of a room disappear, and thus increase its air of comfort.

Seat furniture witnessed the most uninhibited and decorative development of the Biedermeier style; the sofa became the quintessence of Biedermeier. It was the centre of the group of seats in the living-room, where it stood behind the large round table. It encouraged two or three people to sit comfortably, and indulge in conversation; moreover it was high enough for meals to be taken there. It was a sociable piece of furniture, created for a period in which the middle class gained most enjoyment and intellectual stimulation from social life. The sofa combined Louis XVI forms—in particular spirited curves—with the heaviness of the Empire style, although the typical chest shape of that era was not adopted. Its front surface was elaborately decorated: volutes, trumpets, cornucopiae, and also dolphins or swans, were used with great success to articulate the curved fronts of the arm-rests. Palmettes, lotus-flowers and swags filled the apron; upholstery was deep, well-filled, and supplemented by cushions. A special variety particularly characteristic of this middle-class period was the so-called 'Magazine Sofa', whose arm-rests were used to accommodate storage boxes, or drawers.

The sofa almost completely displaced the arm-chair, and the sole piece of seat furniture produced at the same time as the sofa was the side chair, whose seat was always upholstered, though never its back. Occasionally a plain caned frame, this seat rested on square, tapering legs: those at the front were straight, or had a brief curve near the ground; those at the back always curved outwards. Their front curves looked as if they had been bent from the straight. The fact that the seat rail was tenoned into the legs was clearly visible. The back legs extended upwards, and thus formed the side supports of the back. Among the rich variety of backs, the most simple type had its back rail fitted between these supports. More frequently, however, the rail was fixed on top of the supports, and projected laterally over them. The area between the top rail and the lower cross-piece of the back therefore provided an ideal opportunity for decoration. The most common form of ornament in this position was the triple-reed motif, followed by rows of plain rails, joined and curved rails, vase shapes, dolphins and other motifs. Turned decoration was only used in isolated instances, and those in the last few years of the period, although turnery was to determine the appearance of chairs in the post-Biedermeier period, the 1830s and 1840s. Another important factor in the appearance of the Biedermeier chair was the fact that it was only intended to be seen from one viewpoint.

Various small pieces of furniture, which were the subject of an unusual degree of attention, remain to be mentioned. Waste-paper baskets, boot-jacks, lamp-shades, needlework stands, fire-screens and even spittoons were all lovingly elaborated. As the middle class of those days could not afford the luxury of private dressing-rooms, utensils that provided for their daily needs and wants had also to find their place in the living-room and were, as a result, made to match the rest of the furniture.

THREE

Sources of the Style

During the last third of the eighteenth century, and the first third of the nineteenth, artistic forms of expression were dominated by neo-classicism. There was, therefore, an inner relationship between the individual styles of the period, and Biedermeier, as one of these styles, cannot disavow its source—the Empire style that preceded it. It is impossible to imagine Biedermeier isolated from this rigorous style modelled on Roman antiquity. The cabinet-makers who created the Biedermeier style, had their roots in the Empire period, although they tried to reject it.

Large, smooth, undecorated surfaces were already a feature of Empire furniture, but then, in contrast to Biedermeier practice, they were always framed by vigorous mouldings, and so transformed into enclosed forms. The framework-panel system of construction was used more frequently than during the Biedermeier period, and this was primarily for formal reasons, and only secondarily on technical grounds.

Rectangular cubic forms were also an essential feature of Empire furniture, though they were used in a more thoroughgoing manner—and in this there is, again, a critical difference from furniture of the Biedermeier period. Cubes were, in fact, treated as solid bodies with three aspects of approximately equal importance. Decorative motifs on the corners of furniture were thus often used to stress the transition from the front to the sides.

The simple, revealed methods of construction used in Biedermeier furniture were also foreshadowed in the Empire period. But here again there were significant differences. In Empire furniture the constructive instinct of the architect, his obvious sense of the distinction between load-bearing and load-giving members, was a dominant factor. This 'architectural' aspect was of greater importance than the contribution of the craftsman which, in contrast to the Biedermeier attitude, was not recognized as possessing any special virtues.

Numerous individual elements of the Biedermeier style were also adopted from the formal repertoire of Empire. The decorative motifs taken over from antiquity which had been, for the most part, essential elements of the Louis XVI style, remained valid during the Biedermeier period without any significant changes. Bead and cyma mouldings, lions' paws and sphinx heads were really simply part of the basic formal repertoire of neo-classicism as a whole. The lyre, which was so popular, for instance, in the supports of tables or small pieces of furniture, occurred in Empire furniture, but had also already been used in the Louis XVI period. Swans' necks used as arm-rest supports, backward-curving chair-legs, and the projecting top drawer on commodes, were other motifs that Biedermeier furniture took over from the Empire style.

Yet it would be a mistake to consider Biedermeier as a mere derivative of Empire, as an Empire style rendered middle-class, or even emptied of value, as has, up to now, almost invariably been done. The differences, indeed the contrasts, between the two, have been indicated in the account of the basic elements of the Biedermeier style. A few examples may further elucidate the distinction. The creative period of Karl Friedrich Schinkel, the great architect of neo-classicism in Berlin, lasted throughout the Biedermeier period. If two secretaires, both executed from his designs, one dating from 1810 (Plate I), and the other from about 1825 to 1830 (Plate 80), are compared, they will be seen to have all the distinguishing features of the style current at the date they were designed. The late Biedermeier piece is conceived as a flat surface, a mere 'façade', with sides of no interest. The secretaire of 1810, on the other hand, has the effect of a sculptural, three-dimensional monument: rounded corners form a transition between its sides, and the piece is surmounted by a circular bowl which can be viewed from all sides. The 'façade' of the Biedermeier cabinet, however, is not built up in an architectural manner; it is merely a surface to be looked at. The pilasters at its sides have no structural function—they do not even have proper bases of their own, and the space where their bases should be is completely filled by a drawer which is absolutely recognizable as such, and runs right across the piece without any articulation. The pilasters are surrounded by a border. But this is so shallow that it would be wrong to call it a frame. Nor is there any architectural detailing on the pilasters of the Empire secretaire, but these appear convincing as load-bearing elements, and have proper bases of their own. In the later piece there is a flat surface between its pilasters, to which narrow fillets have been applied; they are presumably intended as capitals, but have a completely un-architectural character. The impression given is not so much of a strict columnar order as of a method of articulating a flat surface, which could be changed at will. The earlier piece is a three-dimensional monument, conceived in stone, while the later piece has obviously been constructed of planks. If the latter is also a documented piece executed for the court, to the design of an architect, it displays all the characteristics of the Biedermeier style, in clear contrast to the Empire piece by the same architect.

In Vienna, unlike Germany, Empire was converted into a national style. A secre-taire of about 1810 in the Österreichisches Museum für angewandte Kunst (Plate II) may serve to clarify this point. Ten to fifteen years later, a German Biedermeier cabinet-maker chose it as a prototype for his own creation; this—a secretaire in the Kestner-museum in Hanover (Plate 91)—is an almost literal copy of the Viennese piece and yet, what a difference! The secretaire in Vienna is completely unified in a single tall curved shape; vigorous lions' paws with acanthus leaves are its basis, and from them emerge trumpets, which terminate at the exact height of the transverse member between the fall-front and the top drawer. It is a sculpturally conceived creation of extreme refine-ment. In the Biedermeier reincarnation of this piece the basic oval shape has shallow, curved lions'-paw feet of a schematic character, and is set on a projecting flat base that has been given a distinct separate identity. Its unusual basic shape, which includes an arched sunk panel in the front, is also conceived completely in terms of two dimensions. Finally, the Biedermeier craftsman has given the body of the piece a flat roof. It is no longer dominated by a single comprehensive shape; instead it looks as if a segment-shaped upper section has been added to its flat top.

The Biedermeier chair is, perhaps, a particularly good illustration of the basic con-trast with the Empire style. The Empire chair was constructed as a single unified entity;[1] its back grew naturally out of the top rail, and curved upwards and backwards as a unity. Its front legs were turned, or formally articulated. Its flat surfaces were encrusted with carving, or bronze mounts, even in positions where they caused discomfort to the sitter. Like all Empire furniture the chair was for display, and could be viewed from any angle; in contrast the Biedermeier chair had a single viewpoint, was unassuming and, first and foremost, comfortable.

[1] Cf. Serge Grandjean, *Empire Furniture*, London, 1966, plates 4, 9a, 40a, 47, 49a and 91.

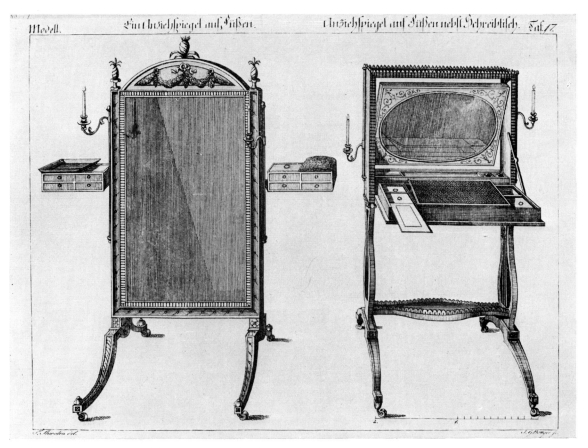

III. THOMAS SHERATON, *Modell- und Zeichnungsbuch für Ebenisten, Tischer, Tapezierer und Stuhlmacher*, Leipzig, 1794,
part III, plate 17, *left*, 'Anziehspiegel auf Füssen nebst Schreibtisch' ('Horse Dressing Glass and Writing Table')
See pp. 51 and 83

The Biedermeier style consciously rejected its predecessor and looked for different models. It had, in fact, virtually no fundamentally common ground with the Empire style. For its basic charm, its stress on comfort and its liking for graceful forms, it was indebted to the first neo-classical style, Louis XVI, or rather primarily to its German version. Small, elegant types of furniture had also been a predilection of that period. Again, the *étagère* was a favourite late eighteenth-century type. Square, tapering legs were another feature of the Louis XVI style which was readopted. Louis XVI chairs also revealed their system of construction in the same way as their Biedermeier successors. The Louis XVI style, which had already used the reed motif on the back-rest, also seems to have inspired the taste for making it richly elaborate.

The secretaire, which enjoyed such wide popularity during the Biedermeier period, was also a favourite Empire form. But the most important precedent for the elaborate and imaginative arrangement of its interior compartments behind the fall-front, often with an element of frivolity, was in Louis XVI pieces of the same type. Biedermeier cabinet-makers also lit upon individual motifs in Louis XVI furniture, such as vase finials, or small balustrades.

The rejection of the formal repertoire of the immediate past, and a reversion to the previous period, are phenomena that can be observed whenever a new style comes into existence. Naturally only those prototypes which satisfy the expressive needs of the present are sought after. Thus it comes as no surprise that Biedermeier cabinet-makers rejected the gilt furniture and richly carved decoration of the Louis XVI period; both were stylistic elements characteristic of a feudal art that seemed to have disappeared once and for all.

In Germany Empire remained a French style. Its rejection by the Biedermeier generation of cabinet-makers may also, therefore, conceal a political motive; French domination had been shaken off, and no one wished to have anything more to do with French art, either of the past, or of the present. Restoration furniture, produced in France at the same time, had no influence on Biedermeier.[1]

[1] Cf. J. Robiquet, *L'Art et le Gout sous la Restauration 1814–1830*, Paris, 1928; Y. Amic, 'Le Mobilier Restauration', *Art et Decoration*, XXI, 1951, p. 24; Y. Brunhammer and M. Ricour, 'Le style Restauration', *Le Jardin des Arts*, 1957/8, p. 121; Y. Brunhammer, *Meubles et Ensembles—Restauration, Louis Philippe*, Paris, 1960.

Attention turned towards a country which was far ahead of the Continent in its economic and industrial development—England. From England came all the important innovations and discoveries, especially the machines, which were greeted with such enthusiasm, and which were soon to influence methods of furniture production. It goes almost without saying, therefore, that the English style of furniture at this time was the third main source on which the Biedermeier style was modelled. From 1815 onwards numerous illustrations of English furniture designs appeared regularly in the *Journal des Luxus und der Moden* that had been published in Weimar since 1785, and was the most widely circulated journal of the period; they largely replaced the illustrations of furniture 'in the Parisian style' that had predominated before that date.

The consistent elaboration of a single display side, one of the most important characteristics of the Biedermeier style, occurred in contemporary English furniture, too, which was also, like Biedermeier furniture, built up of a combination of simple cubic shapes.[1] A few examples may illustrate the extent, on occasion, of the Biedermeier style's debt to England. A sofa in Schloss Charlottenhof in Potsdam (Plate 84) would appear to have been executed from the same design as an English sofa in the Chinese taste of about 1815;[2] arm-rests in the form of an elongated S-curve, and short curved feet are common to both, as is also the exclusively frontal viewpoint. If its Chinoiserie japanning is ignored, the somewhat comical English piece will be seen to have a certain Biedermeier flavour—a reversal of the true facts, which should make the source of the German piece evident. There are also numerous German examples of the type of table with ingenious, if slightly awkward, dolphin-shaped legs on lions'-paw feet, so popular in England, and it is probable that their makers were familiar with English examples (Plate 94).[3]

English cabinet-makers' pattern books had always been celebrated in Germany, a point which will be dealt with shortly. Even 'Michael Angelo Nicolson's *The Practical Cabinet Maker*, of 1826, was not without influence on Biedermeier cabinet-makers, although a German translation did not appear until 1843.[4] Another sofa from Schloss

---

[1] Clifford Musgrave, *Regency Furniture*, London, 1961, plate 8B.

[2] Musgrave, op. cit., plate 26.   [3] Musgrave, op. cit., plate 29.

[4] Michael Angelo Nicholson, *Werkzeichnungen für Zimmerer und Tischler*, translated from the English by F. G. Wieck, and revised by F. E. Conradi, Chemnitz, 1843.

Charlottenhof (Plate 112) must serve as an indication of Nicolson's importance as a source of designs;[1] its vigorously curved arm-rests, elaborate recessed feet, and total stress on a single viewpoint, are the result of stylistic impulses identical to those of Nicolson. Examples can be multiplied at will: small tables with lyre-shaped supports, and extraordinary strongly curved feet;[2] together with tables with folding side-leaves, and curved feet fixed to a flat base ending horizontally, without any transition, in anaemic lions' paws;[3] or small pieces serving as flower-stands or work-boxes, with basket-like containers formed of thin curved rails.[4]

However, contemporary English cabinet-makers' productions, which became known on the Continent through their publication in journals or, especially in North Germany, through direct contact, were not the only models adopted; as had happened in the search for native German models, late eighteenth-century cabinet-makers were imitated as well. A so-called 'Patent Secretaire', a small writing-desk in the form of a fire-screen, by Adolph Friedrich Voigt, a Berlin cabinet-maker (Plates 86 and 87), provides an example; its almost exact model is Plate 17 of Sheraton's *Drawing Book* (Plate III), of which a German translation had been published as early as 1794.[5] The looking-glass on the same plate has the idiosyncratic Biedermeier 'bent' legs. Furniture of the late Sheraton period was often a source of inspiration to German cabinet-makers. The round table with a central column supported on four curved legs, its deep apron fitted with drawers (Plate 69), was introduced to Germany from England.[6] The scallop motif so popular for inlay in North Germany was, as a final example, also English in origin.

The Biedermeier furniture style was, therefore, a river fed by three springs—Empire, Louis XVI and England.

[1] Cf. Musgrave, op. cit., plate 32A.
[2] Musgrave, op. cit., plate 61.
[3] Musgrave, op. cit., plate 62F.
[4] Musgrave, op. cit., plate 66A.
[5] H. Schmitz, 'Ein Berliner Sekretär der Biedermeierzeit', *Berliner Museen, Berichte*, XLVI, 1925, p. 35.
[6] Cf. Ralph Fastnedge, *Sheraton Furniture*, London, 1962, plate 47.

FOUR

Regional Characteristics and Regional Cabinet-makers

VIENNA AND THE KINGDOM OF THE DANUBE

For the Biedermeier style Vienna was the most important metropolis. A large middle-class city, whose court did not have a decisive influence on artistic matters at this date—and, unlike Berlin and Munich, there were no architects of consequence active in Vienna at the time—was bound to become the centre of a middle-class style. Further-more the Viennese middle class was economically secure, and that assured level of prosperity resulted in a demand for the fulfilment of their desire for tasteful comfort.

In the Empire period Viennese cabinet-makers had already created independent forms of their own, in contrast to Germany where Empire remained a French style. Of all the German-speaking capitals Vienna was furthest from Paris, and, despite certain bonds of affinity, never so heavily influenced by France as to lose its independence. Austrian Empire furniture was never characterized by the austerity, and almost repellent coldness, which was peculiar to French furniture of the period. It had a certain likeable quality: its shapes were imaginative, and the fact that it was constructed of wood was not concealed. In Vienna, therefore, more than anywhere else, Biedermeier evolved from the Empire style nearly without a break; it is thus understandable that Viennese cabinet-makers should have created individual and distinctive varieties of Biedermeier furniture.

Contemporary witnesses were thoroughly aware of the high quality of Viennese products. In 1820 Stephan Edler von Keess wrote: 'In general, experts maintain that Viennese furniture bears the closest comparison to French with regard to the taste of its ex-ecution and the beauty of its forms; that the products of the majority of workshops are not as soundly executed as English furniture, but that it sets its own standards in decoration.'[1]

[1] Stephan Ritter von Keess, *Darstellung des Fabriks- und Gewerbewesens im österreichischen Kaiserstaate*, Vienna, 1820, II, p. 96.

In 1816 there were 875 independent cabinet-makers; by 1823 the total had risen to 951. However, a distinction must be made between the 'civic' cabinet-makers, who belonged to the guild, and the 'licensed' cabinet-makers, who were originally licensed by the court to practise their trade. The surprising fact that, during the Biedermeier period, these latter, who did not belong to a guild, were in a large majority (578 in 1816, 620 in 1825) demonstrates the way the crafts were making continual progress in their efforts to liberate themselves from the essentially medieval control of the guilds, with the eventual aim of complete freedom to trade. Some of these cabinet-makers had already started to run regular factories; in the forefront was Josef Danhauser, who was employing well over 100 workmen as early as 1808. Exports of furniture attained an astonishing volume, consistently exceeding imports by a factor of about a hundred.[1] Not only was furniture exported to Hungary, Galicia and Trieste, but also to many of the German states, including far-distant Berlin; indeed it reached France, Turkey and even Russia.

If the Viennese court had no influence in artistic matters, the state in other ways played an important role in the encouragement of the trades. Kaiser Joseph II (1765–1790) had passed a law by which any craftsman, whose trade also demanded skill in draughtsmanship, could only be granted the privileges of a master if he had attended the Akademie der bildenden Künste for a specified period. In 1807, following the advice of his councillors, Kaiser Franz I of Austria (1792–1835) founded a collection of the products of the arts and crafts which was intended to act as an example and inspiration to master craftsmen. In 1815, as a result of Johann J. Prechtl's painstaking planning, and his report of 1810, a polytechnical school was founded; the technical collection attached to this constituted, as it were, a permanent exhibition of industry. As well as scientific, mechanical and technical implements, it contained an official selection of the best and most up-to-date contemporary designs in every branch of the applied arts. The foundation of this institution was an event of far-reaching importance, not only for Vienna and Austria, but also for the whole of Germany.

Viennese Biedermeier furniture is inextricably linked with the name of Josef Danhauser, just as that of his son is inseparable from Viennese painting in the Biedermeier period. Danhauser senior emigrated to Vienna from Württemberg at the beginning of

[1] Keess, op. cit.

the century, and was by profession not a cabinet-maker but a sculptor. An outsider thus becoming the director of an important furniture factory was a momentous event of especial significance for the period, which had many parallels elsewhere. He began his activities in Vienna with the manufacture of carved ornaments as a substitute for bronze mounts. In 1804 he founded his Etablissement für alle Gegenstände des Ameublements in which he sold not only his own furniture but also curtains, carpets, all types of up-holstery, clocks, bronzes and, from 1820, glass as well. The business grew rapidly. In 1807 he was employing eighty workers; by 1808, 130. He continued to produce imita-tion bronze mounts, but soon changed his methods; the ornaments were no longer carved but, instead, formed in moulds from a modelling material. At the beginning of the Biedermeier period Danhauser was running an organization such as, in the oft-quoted words of Keess, 'had never before existed in the Kingdom of Austria, and had its only parallel in the most prosperous period of trade in the Netherlands'.[1] As well as his factory and shop—Auf der alten Wieden—in Vienna, he had a warehouse in Pest. After his death in 1830, his son ran the factory for another eight years before devoting himself entirely to painting.

Only furniture from his own designs was produced in Danhauser's factory; over 2,500 autographed drawings are preserved in the Österreichisches Museum für angewandte Kunst.[2] But a small proportion of these are by his son and these, according to the strict definition of the term adopted here, are no longer designs for Biedermeier furniture. The drawings are kept ready to hand in portfolios, as they were in the factory, so that they could be readily submitted to the customer; they are, therefore, arranged according to type. The variety and quantity produced was remarkable. It included cupboards, dwarf cupboards (so-called 'Garderoben'), commodes, pier commodes, desks, dressing-tables, pier-tables, sofa-tables, work-tables, card-tables, flower-stands, tea-tables, sofas, benches, side-chairs, arm-chairs, garden chairs, children's chairs, exercising chairs, stools, bed-stools, foot-stools, bidets, clothes-baskets, music-stands, canterburies, sideboards, toilet mirrors, spittoons, ash-trays, needlework frames, all types of lamps, pipe-racks, gun-racks, billiard-cue-racks, *étagères*, dumb-waiters, fire-screens, and, finally, altars and pulpits—as well as much besides. Unfortunately not a single drawing

[1] Keess, op. cit., p. 93f.
[2] F. Windisch-Graetz, 'Le bon gout selon M. Biedermeier', *Connaissance des Arts*, 1959, No. XCI, p. 76.

is dated; early and late designs are mixed willy-nilly together. Danhauser's inventive capacity seems inexhaustible: the whole range of Biedermeier forms, from the simplest to the most elaborate, is represented.

However, all Danhauser's designs betray a pronounced feeling for construction. This resulted in the creation of furniture of graceful rectilinearity, without any decoration or curves, whose beauty has a wonderfully timeless simplicity. But such thinking in terms of construction is not only apparent on the technical plane, producing pieces suitable for hand production, but also in pieces that are elaborately formed and full of lively 'movement'. A sofa (Plate 1), whose arm-rests are formed as elongated volutes, provides an example; with radical consistency the larger scrolls at the base of the volutes form its feet, which are made as a single cylinder, extending the whole width of the piece. Nothing is allowed to interrupt the curve of the volutes; the seat and its sides are made to look like a box with curved sides fitted in between them. An exactly similar sofa, which was formerly in a Viennese private collection,[1] and another (Plate 2), whose imaginatively formed stand is probably based on a Danhauser design, provide evidence that such pieces were not merely games on paper. In the latter sofa the seat rail seems to have been bent round at the end of the seat, and turned towards its centre, while tapering off into slender volutes. Danhauser's intellectually conceived form has combined the delight in 'bent' parts, already mentioned as an integral constituent of the Biedermeier style, with the exclusive accent on a single viewpoint, which was also a recurring characteristic. The side-view of the piece has no attraction, especially as its arm-rests are formed of upholstery alone.

Among Danhauser's drawings is a design for a pier commode, whose front, containing seven drawers, is formed as a large curved volute (Plate 3); a piece survives with only slight variations (Plate 4). Its volutes have been executed in an even more radical form than those shown in the drawing; at the bottom they terminate not in lions' paws but, instead, in a second volute which, as on the two sofas, extends as a cylinder across the whole width of the piece. Despite the Biedermeier delight in a 'bent' surface, this piece cannot be denied a certain monumental dignity; it is a clear illustration of how Danhauser's style, typically for Vienna, evolved from Empire.

[1] Josef August Lux, *Von der Empire- zur Biedermeierzeit*, Stuttgart, 7th ed., plate 57.

A drawing of a night table, whose body is sharply tapered towards its base, must serve as a final example of Danhauser's inexhaustible creativity (Plate 5); a night table executed on such a principle may also have been produced in his factory (Plate 6). It at once displays its Empire ancestry, if only in its applied bronze mounts. However, the two disks, on each side beneath the marble top, prove that this piece belongs to the Biedermeier period, as does the significant detail that the round applied moulding underneath the drawer is not continued along its sides.

A night table of a completely different form (Plate 7), whose cupboard is fixed between two slender columns, themselves standing on slightly arched bases, provides an illustration of Danhauser's constructional principles. It is an exceptional demonstration of the desire of this Biedermeier master to reveal all the separate elements of which the piece is compounded. On top of the short body of the cupboard, fixed between the columns, rests a flat box, forming the drawer, also supported by the columns. The front and back of the piece are 'bent' in a shallow curve.

Even plainer is a table of absolutely chaste form, whose quality lies in its simple but sure proportions (Plate 8). It is constructed of planks and squared timbers, and its sole decorative elements, which are scarcely noticeable, are small applied bases round its feet, and dark brown stringing lines round the tops of its legs, which, together with small square applied mouldings round the legs just below the apron, give the impression of a kind of capital. At this period only Danhauser could abstract to such an extent, and create such a 'pure' piece of furniture, reduced to its basic elements. It is pieces of this type which make it understandable that the Biedermeier style was rediscovered and recognized as worthy of imitation in the years from 1910 to 1920.

The collection of drawings in Vienna makes it possible to identify another group of furniture as the work of Danhauser. A lady's oval desk, of which a number of examples have survived, including one originally owned by the Archduchess Sophie, displays all the characteristics of this cabinet-maker;[1] a very similar model exists among the designs. There is also a closely corresponding design for a dumb-waiter, whose shelves are sup-

---

[1] Examples can be found in the Österreichisches Museum für angewandte Kunst, the Bundes-Mobilien-Verwaltung and the Geymüller-Schlösschen. Cf. Rupert Feuchtmüller and Wilhelm Mrazek, *Biedermeier in Österreich*, Vienna, 1963, plate 54, and a drawing by Danhauser (LXXII/1850) in the Österreichisches Museum für angewandte Kunst, Vienna.

ported by widely curving members.[1] In view of the variety of his designs, his enormous creative range, and an output surpassing that of all his contemporaries, many other surviving pieces must have originated in the Danhauser factory. It is tempting to number two tables (Plates 9 and 10) among them, but, as they exhibit general stylistic tendencies common to other cabinet-makers, this can only be put forward as a conjecture.

At this early date Josef Danhauser's factory was probably unique in the whole German-speaking area. The fact that, thanks to the survival of his drawings, his style is so clearly recognizable, must also be taken as a unique piece of luck. Very few other pieces of Biedermeier furniture can be linked with the names of individual makers, although a whole series are mentioned in contemporary accounts. Keess[2] mentions Martin Braun, Martin Schäcker, Ernst Seiffert and Johann Reimann as ranking among the most distinguished cabinet-makers in Vienna. Seiffert sent to the 'National-Fabriks-produkten-Kabinett' a needlework box veneered with elm and decorated with bronze mounts, which was described as extremely tasteful.[3] In W. C. W. Blumenbach's work, *Wiener Kunst- und Gewerbsfreund oder der neueste Wiener Geschmack* (published in Vienna in 1825), a series of pieces by Reimann are illustrated; the examples reproduced are indebted to a surprising extent to the formal vocabulary of the Empire style. In this respect Reimann's son, Friedrich, surpassed his father, as is demonstrated by a little table of elaborate Empire form, signed and dated 1827, in the Bundes-Mobilien-Verwaltung in Vienna.[4] Blumenbach also illustrated furniture by Johann Philipp Hefft, whom he considered one of the best cabinet-makers in Vienna. Hefft also gave drawing lessons to young cabinet-makers, and executed designs for his colleagues. Furthermore, he invented a process for making wood resistant to the effects of humidity and temperature, which was supposed to render superfluous the cross-cut mouldings that had hitherto been the normal practice.

Other Viennese cabinet-makers were also responsible for inventions at this period. In 1828 Felix Goser received a patent for his process for stamping wood in a mould. In

[1] Österreichisches Museum für angewandte Kunst, Vienna. Cf. *Casa d'oro*, II, 1968, p. 668, and a drawing by Danhauser (LIII/1411) in the Österreichisches Museum für angewandte Kunst, Vienna.
[2] Keess, *Darstellung des Fabriks- und Gewerbewesens im österreichischen Kaiserstaate*, Vienna, 1820, II, 93.
[3] *Jahrbücher des k.k. polytechnischen Instituts in Wien*, IV, 1823, p. 61.
[4] Inv. No. HV 1377.

1824 Karl Hirschfeld, a fancy-goods manufacturer, invented a versatile type of decoration for screens, cases, work-boxes and the like, and, in 1828, a '*Granit-Masse*' that could be applied to wood, metal, bone or composition. In the same year Joseph Schwab, the Viennese cabinet-maker's journeyman, obtained his patent for the invention of a method of manufacturing drawers so that they never became stuck, and, even when they were very heavily loaded, could easily be opened and shut. However the main object of production of Schwab's workshop was parquetry, whose quality was praised at the 1845 Vienna Exhibition. Again in 1828, Heinrich Lott, a Pest cabinet-maker, patented a water-proof glue.[1] Finally, in 1832, Mathias Krupnik, a licensed Viennese cabinet-maker, developed his adjustable sleeping-chair. However, not a single piece of furniture by any of these makers has yet been identified.

As early as 1794 Matthias Leistler founded a cabinet-making workshop in Gumpendorf, a suburb of Vienna, which was taken over by his son, Carl, in 1828. But the earliest known pieces by him are those produced from 1842 onwards, as the result of a prestigious commission to furnish the Palais Liechtenstein—thus dating from a time when the Biedermeier style was already a thing of the past.

The name Holl is associated with a series of similar ladies' desks of exceptional elegance (Plate 11). Their extraordinarily rich and imaginative form, together with the masterly quality of their execution, allows these pieces to be recognized as Viennese productions. The cylinder can be opened up to the perpendicular; behind it is an elegant architectural façade incorporating drawers and, at the sides, little doors; the writing flap slides back, and the main drawer is fully fitted for needlework. As well as the illustrated example in Graz Museum, there was a similar desk in the Österreichisches Museum für angewandte Kunst which was, however, destroyed in the Second World War.[2] It was marked with the name 'Holl'. Another similar piece is in Schloss Karlslust in Lower Austria;[3]

[1] *Jahrbücher des k.k. polytechnischen Instituts in Wien*, VIII, 1826, p. 378f.; XII, 1828, p. 324; XIII, 1828, pp. 309 and 376; and XX, 1839, p. 363.

[2] Feulner, *Kunstgeschichte des Möbels*, 3rd ed., p. 747, and Hermann Schmitz, *Deutsche Möbel des Klassizismus*, Stuttgart, p. 129.

[3] Josef Folnesics, *Innenräume und Hausrat der Empire- und Biedermeierzeit in Österreich-Ungarn*, Vienna, 1902, 3rd ed., 1922, plate 47, and Catalogue of *Der Wiener Kongress* (an exhibition held in Vienna in 1965), No. XXI, 4 (I am grateful to Dr F. Windisch-Graetz of Vienna for drawing my attention to this piece of furniture).

the surround of its main drawer is stamped 'B HOLL BDM WIEN'. No other stamped pieces produced in Vienna are known. Curiously enough, though, no cabinet-maker by the name of Holl has yet been identified in the Viennese archives. Indeed, in view of the quality and obvious quantity of his productions, it is frankly baffling that his name never crops up in contemporary literature or exhibition reports. A fourth desk, again unsigned, is in the 'Geymüller-Schlössel' branch of the Österreich-isches Museum für angewandte Kunst.

A work-table of the same type is preserved in the Schloss at Schwetzingen (Colour Plate A). The most marked difference from the pieces at Vienna, Graz and Karlslust is in the arrangement of its legs; they are strongly curved, and between the front and back on both sides are two snakes, which interwine three times, and are pierced by an arrow. Although the piece is not stamped, it seems clearly attributable to Holl. But the collec-tion of drawings in the Österreichisches Museum für angewandte Kunst shows how much caution must be exercised in making such attributions in the Biedermeier period. Thanks to pattern-books and drawing schools, such furniture forms quickly became com-mon knowledge. A drawing of a similar table by Gottlieb Pohl exists,[1] as does another, executed in Carl Schmidt's drawing school, with two examples of this form (Plate 12).

Schmidt was born in 1800 in Soldin, in Prussia, left his home at the age of twenty, spent a number of years in Prague, working as a cabinet-maker's journeyman, and then came to Vienna to study at the Akademie der bildenden Künste under the architect, Peter von Nobile. After completing his studies, he founded a private drawing school, where he taught mainly cabinet-makers, but also all other types of craftsmen. From 1848 to 1858 he was a councillor of the city of Vienna, and he was ultimately appointed an alderman.

Two other drawings executed in his school contain, among other pieces, little globe-shaped work-tables, with tall curved legs (Plate 13).[2] The upper part of the globe can be slid back, allowing access to the interior, which is most attractively partitioned and fitted up; round the globe section of each table is a vertical band inlaid with the signs of the Zodiac. The drawing illustrated here is signed by Carl Schmidt's pupil, Friedrich Paulich.

[1] Hartwig Fischel, 'Möbelentwürfe der Empire- und Biedermeierzeit', *Kunst und Kunsthandwerk*, XXIII, 1920, p. 108.
[2] Fischel, op. cit., p. 107.

An Austrian private collection includes a *Globustischchen* that corresponds almost exactly to Paulich's design, except that the band with the signs of the Zodiac is horizontal and the arrangement of the interior is slightly different (Plate 14).[1] However, it cannot be stated with absolute certainty that Paulich was in fact the author of the surviving piece; it is equally possible that Schmidt used such pieces as models in his school, where they were copied by his pupils, or that he himself was the maker. In any case his pupils' drawings are evidence that the *Globustischchen*, like the ladies' desks attributed to Holl, must have been made towards the end of the Biedermeier period. From what is known of Schmidt's life history he can scarcely have founded his school before 1825, and it can be confidently assumed that he taught and showed his pupils the most modern fashions of the day.

The *Globustischchen* is among the most beautiful and exquisitely made pieces of Biedermeier furniture; the execution of the two hemispheres which fit into one another displays remarkable technical mastery. The mirror-like surface of its exceptionally finely figured yew veneer reflects not merely the cabinet-maker's skill, but also his delight in beautiful materials, which he consciously stressed as such. Its legs, with their lions' paws and lions' masks, reveal their Empire ancestry, but their springy curvature is completely in the Biedermeier spirit. The piece contains scarcely any metal. This charming creation, graceful without being fragile, is a perfect whole, an ornament for any room, as attractive as it is useful.

Thanks to Josef Folnesics' important picture-book, which illustrated a series of pieces executed by him in 1824, the Viennese cabinet-maker, Johann Hertel, is well known;[2] the set comprises a sofa, arm-chairs, side chairs, an oval table with two fluted columnar legs and a pier commode with a small matching cupboard.

Even so, the greater part of Viennese furniture must remain anonymous, and this includes such exceptional pieces as a small lyre-shaped secretaire in Munich (Plates 15 and 16). Here the Viennese delight in radically new forms for this furniture type,

---

[1] Further examples of this type of 'Globustischchen' are in the Museum of Applied Arts in Prague, and the Bayerisches Nationalmuseum in Munich. In my view, two pieces in English collections are also German productions (see Fastnedge, op. cit., plate 52, and Geoffrey de Bellaigue, *Buckingham Palace*, London, 1968, p. 115).

[2] Folnesics, op. cit., plates 13, 14 and 19.

already a familiar feature of the Empire period (Plate II), reappears. Its lyre shape, so favoured at the date, is carried out with such consistency that the strings are executed as beaded mounts (of calibrated width!), on the drawer fronts. The piece is clearly an assemblage of different parts; the base, containing a drawer, formed as a flat rectangular cube, the lyre-shaped upper section, with its fall-front (the three upper drawers are false) mounted on the incurved intermediate section, and a crowning segment, again containing a drawer. Both this segment, and the curved frame of the lyre contain shallow sunk panels, which obtain their decorative effect from the exquisite figure of the wood. The mounts do not stress architecturally significant points but rather accompany the outline of the piece in symmetrical rows. The maker has resolved the usual permutation of pigeon-holes and drawers behind the fall-front in an original manner, by putting a pyramid in the interior (Plate 16).

The drawing by Friedrich Paulich previously mentioned (Plate 13), includes a similar piece in the elaborate late Biedermeier manner, demonstrating how strongly Viennese cabinet-makers favoured the lyre shape for secretaires, and how long the fashion lasted.

Another extremely ingenious shape occurs in a secretaire in Dresden (Plate 17). In this case its upper part, which supports an incurved top section, is formed as a complete circle; the fall-front is like a square drawn in this circle. The fall-front, the intermediate section below it and the top section are the same width, so that an elongated rectangle appears to transfix the circle like a pier. The basic elements of the piece are geometrical shapes attached to and interpenetrating one another, simple cubic forms, sunk panels and beautifully figured wood.

Love of wood is responsible for the surface decoration of a Viennese table, whose unknown maker has fitted together a large number of heterogeneous pieces of veneer in irregular interlocking shapes (Plate 18); particularly noteworthy are its bent-looking legs, which again recall a lyre shape, and seem to interpenetrate the curved sections suspended from the apron. The spandrels under the apron are filled with scallop ornament which, combined with the turned vase on the stretcher, betrays the relatively late date of this piece's manufacture.

A workstand, which originally belonged to Emperor Franz I (Plate 19), provides a further example of the brilliant feeling for construction characteristic of the Viennese cabinet-maker. In this case the side pedestals, that curve outwards at top and bottom, are in fact interpenetrated so that the reading slope can be raised by a concealed ratchet mechanism, allowing it to be used in a standing position.

A large, round table (Plate 20) provides a final example of upward curving detached members; they curve up from the corners of its base to its central pillar, lending a basically solid and weighty piece a pleasing hint of grace. The lions' paws, which are almost abruptly set under these members, illustrate the way in which Biedermeier cabinet-makers used Empire motifs, without integrating them smoothly into the main forms of their pieces. The piece's attraction is increased by the use of choice woods—its top and central pillar of burr birch, its base and the curved members ebonized, and the lions' paws in so-called 'verd-antique' green, a colour intended to resemble patinated bronze.

Vienna must be regarded as a centre of the Biedermeier style; it clearly influenced everything produced in the kingdom of the Danube, although this does not imply that no furniture of high quality or complete originality was produced elsewhere. The products of Bregenz, for example, were especially famous for their remarkably fine polish. In 1823 Joseph Rienzler of Bregenz sent to the Vienna 'National-Fabriks-Produkten-Kabinett' a large writing-box, which was praised for the finesse of its execution.[1] From 1799 Michael Wessicken was active in Salzburg, and in Innsbruck an established tradition must have served as a basis for the work of Johann Nepomuk Geyer at the very end of the Biedermeier period.

In Prague an industrial exhibition of the whole Austro-Hungarian monarchy was held as early as 1791. Four cabinet-makers were represented at the first 'Öffentliche Ausstellung der Industrie-Erzeugnisse Böhmens', in 1829; these were Johann Abbt, Franz Feigl who called himself a furniture manufacturer, Franz Fenner, a fancy cabinet-maker whose walnut secretaire was praised for its pleasing form and good architectural proportions, and Friedrich Röhrs who was given an 'Honourable Mention' for his desk in ebonized pear-wood.[2] This marked the beginning of Röhrs' rise to the status of entrepreneur; in 1834 he obtained official permission to set up a furniture factory, in which he was employing 100 workers as early as 1845. The jury of the exhibition included

[1] Keess, op. cit., p. 95, and *Jahrbücher des k.k. polytechnischen Instituts in Wien*, IV, 1823, p. 91.
[2] *Berichte der Beurteilungs-Commission über die im Jahre 1829 . . . statt gefundene öffentliche Ausstellung der Industrie- Erzeugnisse Böhmens*, Prague, 1831.

the court cabinet-maker and furniture manufacturer, Friedrich Wenzel Kilches, who was to attract attention with his contributions to various exhibitions in the 1840s. A table from Prague (Plate 22) illustrates the city's close relationship with Vienna.[1] Keess described the products of Brünn as 'brav', and most furniture made in Lemberg was exported to Russia; Karlsbad was famous for the charmingly decorated boxes manufactured there, to be bought as souvenirs by those taking the waters.

Hungary too had a close relationship with Vienna (Plate 23). A final example of the extent of Viennese influence is provided by a small work-table from Zagreb, whose ingenious curved legs, gripping a suspended central column, are so influenced by Viennese productions, that it may in fact be a Viennese export piece (Plate 24). A bed from Schloss Opeka in Jugoslavia, on the other hand, is definitely a native production (Plate 25).

MUNICH AND THE KINGDOM OF BAVARIA

The situation in Munich was completely different from that in Vienna. The Munich of the Biedermeier period, and with it the whole of Bavaria, was indelibly stamped by the exceptional personality of its monarch, King Ludwig I, who ascended the throne in 1825, but who had already, as crown prince, exercised a strong influence on architectural activity in his capital city. Ludwig was completely and utterly obsessed by neo-classical ideas and, in 1815, succeeded in persuading Leo von Klenze, the neo-classical architect of Kassel, to come to Munich. The general building plan for the enlargement of Munich, which was drafted as early as 1812, and which provided for the removal of its fortifications, involved building activity on an unprecedented scale, and this was forthwith set into motion. In 1816 were laid the foundation stones for Klenze's Glyptothek, and for the palace of the Duke of Leuchtenberg, Napoleon's stepson. In 1824 the Ministry of War gave the newly-laid-out Ludwigsstrasse its first important building; in 1826 a concert hall, the 'Odeon', was built, and, in the same year, the Residenz was started with the 'Königsbau'.

The neo-classicist Klenze soon realized that classical antiquity could not provide the

[1] Cf. for example a table in the Österreichisches Museum für angewandte Kunst: Peter W. Meister and Hermann Jedding, *Das schöne Möbel im Lauf der Jahrhunderte,* Heidelberg, 1958, plate 540.

model for complete street façades with houses, palaces and administrative buildings. However, he recognized that the Italian towns of the Renaissance had already once faced similar problems of town planning, and thus became the first architect in Germany to experiment with revived Renaissance forms and, therefore, with historicism. However, Klenze's Munich always remained a monarchical city and was not, like Vienna, a middle-class capital; its architecture did not display Biedermeier tendencies, nor was the furniture which Klenze designed for his king in the Biedermeier style. As his great building projects first approached completion in the late 1820s and 1830s, that middle-class style was, in any case, dying out at the time when their interior decoration was being carried out. For the furniture of his palaces he used a rich and sumptuous Empire style, which was also readopted elsewhere at this early stage of historicism.

In the Munich of these years the king's building activities were the all-important factor; the middle class had little opportunity for development, all the more so as Munich had remained a small countrified city.

Nor, as a result, were the self-supporting middle-class crafts encouraged by the Government, but by a private polytechnic, which was formed in 1816 through the initiative of an individual businessman, Karl Zeller. In Germany this was the first of many such associations, which were soon to be founded in increasing numbers: Ansbach followed in 1817, Berlin in 1821, and, by 1830, there were some twenty. Their importance in the evolution of craft into industry is almost inestimable. A year before, in 1815, Zeller had started to publish a *Wöchentlicher Anzeiger für Kunst- und Gewerbefleiss im Königreich Baiern*, in which he publicized all the important contemporary inventions and innovations in craftsmanship, machinery and the applied sciences. His most important innovation was the 'Commissions-Magazin', also founded in 1815, which was intended to assist craftsmen by marketing and testing materials, and to increase sales through a permanent exhibition. He organized regular exhibitions in the main room of a restaurant too. On a larger scale an 'Ausstellung der Kunst- und Gewerbserzeugnisse' was held in 1817, at the same time as the agricultural exhibition at the Oktoberfest, both ventures being repeated in 1818, 1819, 1822, 1823 and 1827.[1]

[1] *Kunst- und Gewerb-Blatt des polytechnischen Vereins im König-Reiche Bayern,* IV, 1818, after col. 696 and col. 777; VI, 1820, col. 17; X, 1824, col. 124; XIV, 1828, col. 193; and *Mitteilungen für Gewerbe und Handel (in Böhmen),* II, 1836, p. 216.

B. CHAIR, probably Franconia, about 1815 to 1820
Cherrywood, decorated with painted stencil ornaments
H. 85, W. 45
Formerly in the Burg, Nuremberg; Stadtmuseum, Munich

Nevertheless, in the years from 1815 to 1830 there was no flowering of craftsmanship. At the exhibition of 1822, for example, a total of only ninety-four objects were sent in by all the crafts, and, at the exhibition of 1823, there was not a single example of cabinet-work. In 1822 there were only forty-four independent cabinet-makers in Munich; in Vienna there were 951! All the same, furniture exports were double the quantity of imports during this period.[1] Thanks to exhibition reports, certain cabinet-makers are known by name.

Franz Fortner (1798–1877), a fancy cabinet-maker, was active in Munich from 1826, and was to carry out large commissions for the Court, especially in the 1830s and 1840s; at the exhibition of 1827 he was publicly commended on 'a beautiful table, executed in various foreign woods, and displaying enormous application'; the comment that he would have gained an even higher award, had he used native woods, is also of interest. Leonhard Glink was not only a cabinet-maker, but the proprietor of a furniture shop as well. In 1828 he was given a licence to set up a wood-drying establishment, but the period of his greatest expansion also began with the 1830s, and thus after the Biedermeier period. At the exhibition of 1818 Michael Heid showed a dressing-table, at which one could write in a sitting or standing position. In 1810, when Johann Georg Hiltl had erected an obelisk on the occasion of the marriage of the Crown Prince Ludwig, he was described in the Weimar *Journal des Luxus und der Moden* as 'the famous furniture manufacturer'. At the Munich exhibitions of 1818 and 1819 he showed furniture with transfer-printed decoration: for example, a secretaire whose fall-front was decorated with a Gothic church revealed, when opened, a church interior, the pigeon-holes and drawers being formed as chapels. Hiltl was the first German to use this ceramic process for furniture decoration; it was, however, a method of ornament most widely used in the 1830s. As well as furniture he produced picture frames, but his speciality was wood-mosaic parquet flooring, made of little squares of cross-cut timber.[2] The cabinet-making firm of Pössenbacher had been established in Munich since the middle of the eighteenth century; in the Biedermeier period Joseph Pössenbacher made all types of furniture, from the simplest to the most elegant, supplied panelling, and everything necessary for

[1] I. Rudhart, *Über den Zustand des Königreichs Bayern nach amtlichen Quellen,* Erlangen, 1827, II, p. 390f.
[2] *Journal des Luxus und der Moden,* Weimar, XXV, 1810, p. 708, and *Kunst- und Gewerb-Blatt des polytechnischen Vereins im König-Reiche Bayern,* IV, 1818, col. 807; V, 1819, cols. 48 and 197.

interior decoration, and also kept a shop with a comprehensive stock of furniture. Joseph Prestel showed a writing-desk at the exhibition of 1818. In 1815 Joseph Reichlmayr exhibited his masterpiece, another desk, in cherry-wood with burr veneer, in Zeller's shop, with the result that it was bought by the king. Benedikt Stuber sent a mahogany secretaire with columns and gilt decoration to the exhibition of 1818. In the following year N. Scherpf sent another mahogany secretaire, decorated with a temple.

Unfortunately it has, so far, proved impossible to identify a single piece of furniture dating from the Biedermeier period by any one of these makers.

The situation of the Munich cabinet-making trade during the Biedermeier period, as outlined above, makes it difficult to distinguish an independent Munich style of Biedermeier furniture. Characteristic of the completely neo-classical ideals of the Court is a secretaire from the Residenz at Munich (Plate 28). It has two writing surfaces, so that one can work at it in a sitting or standing position. Its heavy proportions and vigorous columns speak the language of Empire; however, the large arch underneath, applied pilasters, projecting mouldings typical of cabinet-makers' work, and hemispherical feet, are Biedermeier elements, which leave no doubt as to when it was made. A writing-desk also from the royal collection displays formal similarities, and may perhaps be by the same cabinet-maker (Plate 29).

The noble simplicity of form of two cupboards in the collection of the Princes of Thurn and Taxis (Plate 30) argues for their having been made at the beginning of the Biedermeier period. They are constructed of completely smooth planks, and their exquisitely graceful decoration consists of representations of Virtues, putti with festoons and laurel-wreaths, an acanthus border that creates the illusion of narrow panels, and an egg-and-dart moulding in the cornice—all printed on the wood. As Johann Georg Hiltl pioneered printed decoration on furniture in the early part of the Biedermeier period, and as his printed ornaments were renowned for the large area they covered, it seems logical to attribute these two cupboards to him.

Simple grandeur is again apparent in the form of the secretaire in Plate 31; its lower section includes another large arch motif in the form of a sunk panel. The fact that its base and pilasters are constructed of planks is openly revealed. Its upper section is flanked by robust untapered columns, and is surmounted by a top section with a graceful cyma recta outline. A similarly shaped top section is found on two further secretaires, which were also originally in the Bavarian royal collection,[1] so that this feature may perhaps be considered the speciality of a particular Munich cabinet-maker.

A bookcase with glazed door-panels, articulated by graceful tracery (Plate 32) also belongs to this group of simple pieces made in Munich; the simple intersecting bars of its tracery lie on the same level as its door-frames, and their exclusive function is to fill its flat front panels. Its simple form is also the basis of the charm of a round table with idiosyncratically curved legs, and four stretchers, which curve upwards in the centre to support two disks (Plate 33). Similar curved legs occur on a narrow console table, sparingly decorated with applied ebonized mouldings (Plate 34).

Simple forms that for all their austerity, have a certain nobility, would seem to constitute the specific character of furniture made in Munich. A table, whose ponderous central column is carried by three comical dolphins (Plate 35), serves to demonstrate that more elaborate forms too were used in Munich; it is, however, the work of a carver, rather than of a cabinet-maker.

Cabinet-makers in Augsburg could look back to a period of exceptional prosperity, and a consistently high level of virtuosity, which had lasted since medieval times, and particularly since the Renaissance; this tradition seems to have continued uninterrupted in the Biedermeier period. In 1822 there were fifty-two independent cabinet-makers in Augsburg; that is, in fact, eight more than in Munich.[2] From 1818 onwards the Kunst- und Zeichnungsanstalt extended their annual exhibitions to include decorative art products. In 1818 the 'Gesellschaft zur Beförderung vaterländischer Industrie' in Nurem- berg also organized an exhibition of art and industry; in 1822 there were seventy-nine independent cabinet-makers in this city and, in addition, G. H. Bestelmeier ran a department store that included everything for interior decoration, ranging from furni- ture, mirrors and chandeliers, to childrens' toys. He regularly sent out printed cata- logues of his stock, and numbered members of the higher aristocracy among his clientele; thus, for example, the *Süddeutsche Zeitung* of 4 October 1838 was able to report that the Tsar's heir had made some purchases from Bestelmeier. A number of cabinet-makers from Regensburg, where there were twenty-seven in 1822, are known by name, and the same, of course, applies to every town, large or small, in the country; at the same time

[1] Munich, Stadtmuseum, inv, no. 35/2165, and Munich, Residenzmuseum, photo No. IX f 28.
[2] Rudhart, op. cit., p. 390f.

there were twenty-five cabinet-makers in Bamberg, seventeen in Bayreuth, and ten in Hof.[1]

The chair in Plate 36, one of a set now in Augsburg Museum, was certainly made in Augsburg, and the whole tradition of this artistic centre is reflected in its simple elegance. The elaborate decoration of its back, executed in stamped brass sheet, shows Apollo and Mercury as patrons of the Muses.

A bookcase from the town hall at Regensburg (Plate 37) must be the work of a cabinet-maker of that city; the ebonized astragals of its glazed upper section are formed as reeds, but also incorporate two crossed keys—the crest of Regensburg. The deeply sunk lower door panels of this piece are an exceptional feature, and the resultant frame does not occur elsewhere in Biedermeier furniture.

A commode (originally in the palace at Eichstädt, not very far from Regensburg) which belonged to the Duke of Leuchtenberg, Napoleon's step-son and King Max I of Bavaria's son-in-law, has frames of a darker veneer round its drawers (Plate 38). Similar frames are a feature of a cupboard in Regensburg Museum (Plate 39), while the exceptionally fine decoration of its outer frame, inlaid in black composition, is modelled on pattern prints published in Kassel in 1818 by J. C. Ruhl.[2] This cupboard exemplifies the high quality of which even cabinet-makers in provincial towns were capable.

In a secretaire in the Schloss at Regensburg, the frame of the lower section again forms an attractive feature. The sides of the frame are decorated with attenuated zig-zag stringing lines, displaying remarkable craftsmanship (Plate 40). Sunk panels, like those on the bookcase in Regensburg Town Hall (Plate 37), occur again in a secretaire in Schloss Ellingen, whose tripartite top section is influenced by Louis XVI furniture (Plate 41); another interesting feature of this piece is the use of a seventeenth-century Italian scagliola panel which is let into the exterior of its fall-front. That this example of the decorative art of an earlier epoch has been adopted and incorporated into this piece is an early indication of historicist thought and sentiment.

The articulation and division of flat surfaces by frames, remarked on all these pieces, whether formed by sunk panels, projecting doors or drawers, or different coloured veneers, would seem to be a feature peculiar to Biedermeier furniture made in Central Franconia, and the Upper Palatinate.

[1] Ibid.

[2] J. C. Ruhl, *Ideen zu Verzierungen für Künstler und Handwerker, aus denen Antiken gesammelt*, Cassel, 1818.

A sofa in Regensburg Museum (Plate 42) is a product of this local style, too, and its use of motifs that are obviously Empire in origin, although they have been transformed into Biedermeier in a vigorous, if naïve, manner, recalls the secretaire in the Schloss at Regensburg (Plate 40).

A bookcase in Bamberg in Upper Franconia (Plate 43) owes much to the style of the late eighteenth century; it was in the collection of Heinrich Joachim Jäck (1777–1847), a Cistercian, who was librarian of Bamberg Library from 1803 onwards. The gallery and vases surmounting it appear to have been taken over without alteration from the formal repertoire of the Louis XVI style; however, its lions'-paw feet, the surface treatment of the front of its lower drawers, the thin board-like pilasters and the flat lattice of bars in front of the glass are conclusive evidence that the cupboard dates from the Biedermeier period. Obvious echoes of Louis XVI furniture have also already been noted in the secretaire from Ellingen (Plate 41).

MAINZ AND THE SOUTH-WEST

Already in the eighteenth century Mainz had an exceptionally progressive cabinet-makers' guild and, as a result, the quality of craftsmanship was remarkably high. The tradition then created continued unbroken into the nineteenth century and, in fact, special circumstances gave it a further impetus; in 1792, as a consequence of the French occupation, the guilds were abolished and complete freedom to trade was established. As a result their restrictive powers, which were often a barrier to progress, especially by impeding the immigration of foreign master-craftsmen, were destroyed, and the limit to the number of journeymen allowed to any single master, a normal feature of the guild system, was waived. There was therefore every opportunity for successful economic development; numerous foreign cabinet-makers moved to Mainz, and a number of large-scale concerns were established.

In 1780 there were 58 independent cabinet-makers in Mainz, with a total of 92 journeymen; by 1815 there were 130 cabinet-makers and, in 1816, as many as 188 with 217 journeymen.[1] As early as 1810 it was reported that the Mainz fancy-cabinet-makers

[1] R. Hirsch, *Die Möbelschreinerei in Mainz, Untersuchungen über die Lage des Handwerks in Deutschland,* Leipzig, 1895, vol. III.

were achieving good sales at the market in Frankfurt and abroad;[1] towards the end of the Biedermeier period, and even more so in the subsequent years, their exports went to Holland, Belgium and England, and even as far afield as Russia and America. It was almost a matter of course for prosperous engaged couples from Frankfurt and Mannheim, Darmstadt and Wiesbaden, even from Karlsruhe and Stuttgart, to travel to Mainz to order their household goods there.

By the end of the 1820s two veneer-cutting machines, procured from Paris, had been installed in Mainz; these made it feasible to use the splendid burr veneers, which it had previously been impossible to cut by hand. At first the wood was brought from the nearby Odenwald, but it was later imported in large quantities from the Italian-speaking region of Switzerland. The reputation of furniture made in Mainz in the nineteenth century was founded principally on three names—Knussmann, Kimbel and Bembe. Johann Wolfgang Knussmann (1766–1840) founded his furniture workshop, which lasted until 1874, in about 1790; already in 1805 more than eighty people were employed there. His most important commission in this early period was the complete furnishing of a bedroom for Napoleon.[2]

Having travelled to Vienna as a journeyman, Wilhelm Kimbel (1786–1869) opened a workshop in Mainz in 1815; his productions were described as 'novel', and as 'admirable in execution and decoration'—doubtless thanks to his training in Vienna. He sent regular contributions to the market at Frankfurt, and was commissioned to fit out the assembly room in Bad Homburg.[3] By means of three pattern-books, which were published in numerous instalments from 1835 onwards, he exercised a significant and far-reaching influence on furniture production throughout Germany during the period subsequent to Biedermeier.

Philipp Anton Bembe, born in 1799, followed his father and grandfather as an upholsterer. While they had only dealt in furniture, he set up his own furniture factory in 1835, which soon enjoyed such a great reputation that it supplied most of the German courts.[4]

[1] H. Brühl, *Mainz*, 1818, p. 343.
[2] Extract from a MS history of the Kaehler family by R. Busch.
[3] Thieme-Becker, *Künstlerlexikon*.
[4] R. F., 'Die Chronik des Hauses Bembé', *Parkett-Industrie und Handwerk*, XI, 1962.

Due to the survival of the autograph drawings for their masterpieces another three of the large number of Mainz cabinet-makers are known by name.[1] Kaspar Schwarz (1781–1840) was the son of a cabinet-maker and his own son followed the same trade; Kaspar Schwarz passed the examination to become a master-craftsman in 1814. His masterpiece was a cylinder desk with a tall tripartite top section; it was an exceptionally plain piece with all the characteristics of the Biedermeier style. Simplicity of form was also a feature of the masterpiece of Franz Himmler (1785–1838), who took the examination a year later. He designed another cylinder desk, with a fall-front in its upper part for working at in a standing position; it had columns on each side, while the drawers below were flanked by pilasters. The masterpiece drawing of Heinrich Bayerlein (1788–*c.* 1845), dated 1816, shows a secretaire with doors below and a flush fall-front flanked by columns extending its full height. These strikingly simple forms, characteristic of furniture made in Mainz, were a decisive influence on the whole of the south-west from the middle Rhine to the lake of Constance. A further drawing must serve as an example; it shows a commode, a night table, and a washing commode, designed by Franz Storck of Offenbach am Main in 1830 (Plate 47). Two more commodes, one in Schloss Meersburg (Plate 48), and the other in the Rosgarten-museum at Konstanz (Plate 49), are an excellent illustration of this simple type—a smooth undecorated chest on square feet, its drawers flanked by ebonized columns. A pier commode, with seven drawers in its smooth chest section, which rests on short tapered legs (Plate 50), also displays almost total simplicity.

A secretaire from Speyer (Plate 51) is more elaborate in form: its base curves gracefully upwards, columns are placed diagonally at its corners and its curved top section is flanked by two powerful S-shaped volutes. Nevertheless, the dominant feature of this piece, too, is its basic modesty, which allows the beautifully grained wood to make the strongest impression.

Chairs were also simple, with horizontally curved back-rests, and reed decoration so formalized as to be almost unrecognizable (Plates 52 and 53), or with backward-curving backs, and inset fretwork decoration in great variety (Plates 54 and 55).

Rather more elaborate in form were sofas, their arm-rests often decorated with cornucopiae, lotuses or the ever popular dolphins (Plate 56).

[1] F. Arens, *Die Meisterrisse und Möbel der Mainzer Schreiner,* Mainz, 1955, plates 104ff.

A container for letters or needlework from Schloss Schwetzingen (Plate 57) illustrates the superlative skill in execution that was also characteristic of cabinet-makers in the south-west. Its egg-shaped body, with a lid of complex interpenetrating forms, looks as if it had been slid, in a most ingenious manner, between the bent legs; all its surfaces are veneered with finely knotted yew-wood, partly in narrow bands separated by dark stringing lines.

In 1829 there was, in the Grand-Duchy of Baden, a total of 2,471 cabinet-makers, with 1,198 journeymen.[1] One of the more important cabinet-makers was the Schwetzingen court cabinet-maker, Rummer, whose father had worked with Roentgen; at the Karlsruhe exhibition of art and industry in 1823 he showed two richly inlaid tables. Contemporary criticism of these two pieces is extremely interesting for the insight it affords into Biedermeier artistic intentions. According to the official report on the exhibition, 'although such work is meritorious in that it displays industry and artistic taste, I maintain nevertheless that one should not strive to imitate painting in wood; in such inlaid works the hand, in trying to produce a painterly effect, has, virtually, to strive after the impossible, while neither the eye nor good taste are satisfied.' For inlaid decoration this critic preferred geometrical forms, or, at most, 'Arabesken à la grecque'.[2] There was therefore a complete rejection of all pictorial inlay, and dependence on the decorative motifs of Louis XVI furniture.

In Rastatt, Eigler was the third generation of his family to act as court cabinet-maker. In Freiburg the bishop's throne, choir stalls and altars were executed by Josef Glänz, a cabinet-maker and carver, who was employed on the restoration of the cathedral from 1820 onwards; in 1829 he was awarded a silver medal at the Karlsruhe exhibition of industry.

THE NORTH GERMAN COASTAL REGION

Biedermeier, as a middle-class style, was also, of its very nature, primarily a South German style; its 'capital' was Vienna, and not the North German Hanseatic towns,

[1] W. L. Volz, *Gewerbskalender für das Jahr 1834*, Karlsruhe, 1834, p. 20.
[2] K. Nehrlich, *Über die Kunst- und Industrie-Ausstellung für das Grossherzogtum Baden von 1823 zu Karlsruhe*, p. 46f.

which, with their middle-class constitutions, might seem to have been predestined for that role. However, with their mayors taking the place of monarchs, and middle-class senators acting as members of the Government, they afforded no opportunity for the reaction against everything involved with court life that was a not unimportant factor in the evolution of Biedermeier. In fact their prosperous merchants had already, in the second half of the eighteenth century, developed a completely independent style, a restrained and massive version of the Louis XVI style, with an English stamp to it. The Empire style never gained a foothold in the Northern towns. The annexation of the Hanseatic towns into the French Empire for the brief three years from 1810 to 1813 was felt as a forcible occupation and, for this reason, liberation produced no reaction to the Napoleonic style. In the North the Southern tendency to revert to the forms of the Louis XVI style took the form of a continuing use of that style, although its motifs were changed, and even came indirectly to include Empire forms. The influence of England, a country with which North Germany had always been in sympathy, also remained strong, and, as a result of extensive commercial links with England, more mahogany was used in North Germany than anywhere else; even the cheapest varieties, sent to the ports as packing material—the so-called 'sugar-chest wood'—were converted into furniture.

In the Focke Museum in Bremen are preserved some drawings by Wilhelm Hemcker (1802–1874), a cabinet-maker who worked in this Hanseatic town. His design for a secretaire, dated 1828, shows a typical piece of North German Biedermeier furniture (Plate 58). It is strictly cubic in form, with, even at this late date, no external applied decoration of any kind, and has a tripartite top section with a raised centre; only in the interior, behind its fall-front, are little columns and inlaid architectural motifs to be found. A design for a secretaire with a cylinder top dating from the following year shows a somewhat richer type of top section (Plate 59); its doors, flanked by small columns, contain horizontally set oval sunk panels, while its stepped upper part, again with a raised centre, is decorated with a scallop motif typical of North Germany. It is instructive to compare the needlework holder from Schloss Schwetzingen (Plate 57) with a wine-cooler from Bremen (Plate 60)—the latter, incidentally, a typically upper-middle-class piece of furniture never found in South Germany. The interval of time between the two is evident; the piece from Bremen displays late Biedermeier stylistic features in its elegantly curved legs, formed as elongated ogees with volutes at their tops; but that is not the only difference between these two small pieces. The body of the North German wine-cooler is a strictly rational construction, formed of eight undecorated flat sections, and a base set on its legs. Its lid has a flat top which overhangs slightly at the edges—no curves, no body slid between bent legs, nor any elaborately interpenetrating forms in its lid, as found in the South German piece.

In 1831 Hamburg was expressly named as one of the centres of German furniture production.[1] A linen cupboard now in the Museum für Kunst und Gewerbe is a superlative example of furniture produced there (Colour Plate D). The fact that its front is divided like a secretaire with a downward folding fall-front is typical of the Biedermeier approach; these horizontal divisions are in fact only simulated on the front, and both square panels can be opened as doors. The reason for this was, once again, shortage of space; the linen cupboard had to be put into a living-room, where it could not be allowed to be recognizable as such. The cupboard is simple, and constructed entirely of flat surfaces; only its top section incorporates richer ornament; in an ebonized semi-circular sunk panel, a typical shape in the whole of North Germany, and also in Scandinavia, is neo-classical painted decoration; it is flanked by two diamond-shaped sunk panels painted with trophies of musical instruments, which would appear to have been borrowed direct from the Louis XVI formal repertoire. The emphatic top of this piece, with its flat pediment, is surmounted by a box-like additional section—another example of the combination of basic geometrical elements characteristic of Biedermeier.

Although somewhat later in date, a mahogany bookcase displays even more of that elegant restraint typical of Biedermeier furniture made in the Hanseatic towns (Plate 61). It is significant that, in this piece, logical consistency in the application of constructional principles is carried to such an extent that its top section is made to look like a continuation of the basic cube of the case, and the strip masking the join between the doors is extended over the lower drawer.

An unusually large corner cupboard from Lübeck illustrates the way in which Empire elements were sometimes incorporated into North German Biedermeier furniture (Plate 62); flat ebonized pilasters with Egyptian bases and capitals flank its top part, the largest,

[1] Bericht über die Ausstellung sächsischer Gewerb-Erzeugnisse im Jahre 1831, Dresden and Leipzig, 1832.

and ebonized bands covered with gilt bronze ornaments provide terminal features at top and bottom. Its grandeur is not due to its external dimensions—ten feet, alone; it is a mixture of genuinely aristocratic feeling and middle-class reticence. Its economy of means acts as a positive virtue. The separate sections are clearly distinguished from one another in the Biedermeier manner. Characteristic of North German Biedermeier furniture is the fluted ornamental motif which radiates, like a fan, from a centre point to its two front feet.

A commode which also comes from Lübeck, with flanking ebonized columns, a shallow curved sunk panel in its base, and a similar diamond-shaped panel in its upper section, is completely free of any reminiscences of Empire or Louis XVI (Plate 63). Its base, and its upper section which is supported by the two columns and which again looks as if it had been pushed through the cornice, are both cube-shaped; the central section with its two drawers, on the other hand, is curved forward.

Seat furniture from the Hanseatic towns, too, displays all the characteristics of the Biedermeier style (Plate 64), curved back-rests with rudimentary volutes or formalized sheaves of reeds serving to fill the back panel. But the chairs also possess a quality of simple elegance which can ultimately be traced back direct to English influence; the inlaid shell in the centre panel of the left-hand chair is a direct borrowing from England.

Schleswig-Holstein was still part of Denmark at this stage, and it is difficult to distinguish furniture made in cities like Schleswig and Flensburg from that made elsewhere in Denmark. A secretaire in Flensburg Museum (Colour Plate C) is influenced by Danish prototypes of the Louis XVI and Empire periods, and the arrangement of its lower section—its sole decoration a delicate band of inlay and sparingly used bronze mounts, very much in the style of the Danish architect, C. F. Harsdorff[1]—has a noble sense of scale. The tripartite top section, with its curved pediment, occurs in Danish secretaires produced from the beginning of the nineteenth century onwards,[2] but the way in which the side sections are attached, the shallow applied pilasters, and the shallow diamond-shaped sunk panel, are clear indications that it was produced during the Biedermeier period.

[1] Cf. E. Lassen, *Danske Møbler, Den klassiske Periode*, Copenhagen, 1958, plate 3.
[2] Cf. T. Clemmensen, *Danske Møbler*, Copenhagen, 4th ed., 1963, p. 75; H. Hayward, *World Furniture*, London, 1956, plate 1000; and E. Lassen, op. cit., plate 39.

A form of commode common in both Schleswig-Holstein and Denmark is illustrated by Plates 65 and 66; it was relatively narrow, with three distinct drawers, unified by their architectural arrangement; the centre drawer contained an arched sunk panel, and the top one a similar diamond-shaped panel.[1] The entirely rectangular example in Flensburg Museum (Plate 65) must have been produced a little earlier than the commode in the Schleswig-Holsteinisches Landesmuseum, with its short curved feet (Plate 66).

The sofa incorporating storage space, which was a typical piece of Biedermeier furniture, was also produced in North Germany (Plate 67). This example's apron contains a large drawer that extends the full width, and its right arm rest incorporates a needlework box for the lady of the house, while the left contains a complete smoker's outfit for the gentleman. The influence of the Danish tradition is again reflected in the heaviness of its form, and the gentle curve of the front of its armrests.[2]

The lyre, that popular motif in the South, was also used in the North, most frequently in small pieces (Plate 68). In this example the classical musical instrument is reproduced with such apparent exactitude that its curves and scrolls do not detract from the austerity of the general structure; it preserves its air of cool distinction, typical of North German furniture, and its delicate stringing lines of chequer inlay contribute further to this effect. In the centre of its top is an inlaid scallop motif.[3]

Because of geographical proximity, active trading connections and spiritual affinities, which were the subject of continual comment, the furniture produced in Schleswig-Holstein and Denmark was influenced by England to a much greater extent than that made in the South. A significant example of the influence is provided by a round table with four high curved legs, a central pillar and a deep apron containing drawers (Plate 69); in this piece, however, the Sheraton prototype[4] has been transformed into something purely Biedermeier by the conversion of its central column into a massive baluster, and by a slight increase in scale in all the individual parts.

As a result of a trade exhibition organized in Schleswig in 1829 the names of a few

[1] Cf. Hayward, op. cit., plate 997.
[2] Cf. Lassen, op. cit., plate 27, and Clemmensen, op. cit., p. 73.
[3] Cf. a similar piece of Danish furniture in Clemmensen, op. cit., p. 76.
[4] Ralph Fastnedge, *Sheraton Furniture,* London, 1962, plate 47.

Schleswig cabinet-makers are recorded:[1] J. Jansen exhibited a secretaire, a sofa and a chair; H. Keck a secretaire, a table and a mirror; W. E. A. Kiöbe a round table; and the cabinet-maker Prien a ladies' desk, two sofa tables and two dining-tables.

A considerable amount of furniture was produced in the city of Altona—now a suburb of Hamburg, but, until 1864, a thriving Danish port. To meet customs regulations this furniture was identified with a mark stamped in sealing-wax, and furniture with traces of such marks is found all over Schleswig-Holstein and Denmark. The mark bore the words '*Altonaer Fabrick Waaren Stempel*', together with the current royal arms of Denmark. The practice of marking Altona furniture in this manner ceased in 1853.[2]

Owing to limitations of space it is not possible to consider here the contemporary furniture made elsewhere in Scandinavia, although much of it betrays strong German influence. This is particularly so of that produced in Denmark, Norway and southern Sweden. The reader is referred to the works of Tove Clemmensen, Ernst Fischer, Erik Lassen, J. H. Lexow and Sigurd Wallin for further information on these aspects of Northern Biedermeier.

The Duchy of Oldenburg, west of Bremen, was also annexed by the French Empire in 1810, but a restoration took place in 1813, and the state was raised to a Grand-Duchy in 1815. The furniture produced in its capital city in the Biedermeier period has a close stylistic relationship to that produced in Schleswig-Holstein. A drawing of a secretaire (Plate 73) executed in 1826 by F. C. Trenter, an Oldenburg cabinet-maker, shows a smooth basic shape, slightly tapering towards its top, fronted with a shallow façade built up of a combination of simple geometric shapes, as in the commode in Plate 65. A conspicuous feature of this piece is a semi-circular sunk panel reoccurring on a design for a secretaire by Johann Bernhard Spanhake, which also contains, in two positions, the elongated diamond-shaped sunk panel (Plate 74). Both examples are drawings for masterpieces. Spanhake, incidentally, joined the Oldenburg trade association in 1840, and was a member of the reviewing commission for the trade exhibition of 1842. Ernst Linck sat his master-craftsman's examination in the same year as Spanhake, and also exhibited in 1842.[3] A sofa table with folding leaves on each side, and a sofa, possibly

---

[1] *Königlich priviligierter Schleswig-Holstein-Lauenburgischer Gewerbsfreund*, II, 1829, cols. 529ff.

[2] See T. Clemmensen, *Møbler paa Clausholm, Langesø, Holstenshuus*, Copenhagen, 1946, pp. 146–52.

[3] *Verhandlungen des Oldenburgischen Gewerbe- und Handels-Vereins*, 1841, p. 90; 1843, p. 252ff.

from the royal collection (Plates 75 and 76) are further examples of perceptible English influence, while a bed (Plate 77) contains Empire elements. Even so, the latter is a Biedermeier piece; its modest and two-dimensional character has nothing in common with the dynamic spatial effects produced by luxurious Empire beds.

A secretaire with an elaborate upper section in Schloss Cappenberg shows a similar use of bronze mounts to those on the bed, indubitably influenced by Empire models (Plate 78); its lower section repeats the form of North German commodes, in which a round arch is applied to the completely square basic shape of the piece, without any regard to its drawers. Above the desk section with its diamond-shaped sunk panel, the upper part is exceptionally elaborate in form, with half rotundas at each side decorated, as is the central door, with mirrors.

BERLIN

The situation in Berlin was comparable to that in Munich. Admittedly the King of Prussia, Friedrich Wilhelm III, has not gone down in history as a strong ruling personality, although his armies won brilliant victories in the wars of liberation. However, his activities in the field of home affairs, his reorganization of the Prussian state, and his restoration of its finances, were of great significance for the people during the Biedermeier period. Much building was being carried out in Berlin. During the years 1816 to 1818 Karl Friedrich Schinkel built the Neue Wache, a building which was completely classical. He followed this with a theatre during the period from 1818 to 1821, which played a large part in the creation of a new architectural style; its side walls owed nothing to the classical language of architecture, and it represented the first German example of a pure skeleton building, built up of openly revealed constructional elements. The Altes Museum of 1822 to 1828 was ultimately followed in 1832 to 1835 by the Bauakademie, a completely functional structure that no longer had anything to do with neo-classicism in the sense of imitation of the architecture of classical antiquity; it was the realization of the Biedermeier structural spirit in the field of architecture.

In Berlin therefore, as in Munich, there was substantial building activity, and an architect with a strong personality. Schinkel, like Klenze, also made furniture designs;

but, whereas Klenze worked exclusively for the court, and designed his royal furniture in the Empire style, Schinkel was far more of an innovator. His architecture reflected a striving after new stylistic principles, and his furniture shows his development into a complete master of the Biedermeier style. In his furniture for the court, it is true, he used the forms of Roman antiquity: originals from Herculaneum and Pompeii can be identified. But there exist in addition pieces based on his designs that are pure Biedermeier in style.[1] His preparatory drawings were very exact, and precisely detailed; indeed, as G. F. Waagen wrote in 1844, he drew 'special patterns for his cabinet-makers, so that they should not fail to achieve the required delicacy in his mouldings'.[2] In 1863 Alfred von Wolzogen gave an account of the extent of his influence on the decorative arts in the Berlin of those days: 'If one goes into any of the older and more important furniture workshops, or manufactories of bronzes, carpets, stoves, ceramics, or silks, and if one asks the leading tradesmen in the capital, one can still hear, from the mouths of their grateful sons, that it was Schinkel who first aroused and refined the formal taste of their fathers, who most generously provided them with designs, and who elevated their previously commonplace crafts to a higher level.'[3]

The situation in Berlin at the beginning of the Biedermeier period was thus complex in the extreme. On the one hand, there had been an independent tradition of cabinet-making since the eighteenth century, and a large quantity of furniture in the Empire style was produced during the early nineteenth century; on the other, royal buildings were commissioned under the direction of a great neo-classical architect, who, nevertheless, found inspiration for new forms of expression in his very neo-classicism.[4] New was compounded with old, aristocratic with middle-class. A character typical of this period was Johann Gottlob Thielemann, a cabinet-maker, who in 1801 entered into a partnership with Loos, the master of the mint, to set up a factory for quality furniture; the ultimate aim of this factory was to execute all kinds of fine cabinet work in native woods exclusively. Until the Second World War the Märkisches Museum in Berlin

[1] Sievers, *Die Möbel* (Schinkel), plates 21, 93, 114, 115, 118, 121, 122, 127, 176, 177, 180, 181, 182 and 222.
[2] G. F. Waagen, 'Carl Friedrich Schinkel als Mensch und als Künstler', *Berliner Kalender,* 1844, p. 367.
[3] A. von Wolzogen, *Schinkel als Architekt, Maler und Kunstphilosoph*, Berlin, 1864, p. 44.
[4] Schinkel was also caught up in the romantic tendencies of his epoch, and designed some important buildings in the Gothic style, some of which were executed, while others were not (they were often alternative designs); others still are to be found in his paintings.

possessed an Empire secretaire by Thielemann that clearly illustrated this nationalistic character of Empire furniture produced in Berlin, which manifested itself in other ways than the use of native woods.[1] The character of Biedermeier secretaires produced in Berlin is illustrated by a splendid example in the Kunstgewerbemuseum in Berlin-Köpenick (Plate 79).

It has a simple basic shape with virtually unarticulated sides, but with a richly elaborated front. Columns set on a diagonal are attached to this basic shape, although they do not fulfil any significant architectural function; they are accessories, corner decoration, and, therefore, dispensable. The articulation of the lower section of the piece is similar to that found on North German commodes; a shallow suggestion of architecture applied to the front of the simple overall shape, forming an arch over the drawers, without creating niches, or a truly architectural vault. As always in Biedermeier furniture the veneer is carried without a break over all this articulation. The top section of the piece is no mere crowning finial but another functional cupboard; its temple-like façade, though superbly executed in every detail, is not a spatially conceived piece of architecture. It is rather another form of surface ornament; both its small columns and its panels look as if they could be slid aside. The top edge of the piece is not formed by the pediment of the temple but by the horizontal line which terminates the cupboard. The arrangement of the interior has a similar character; its four small columns are set too far apart to form an order in the classical sense, and paintings are set between them at each side, thus converting the columns into frames. The niche between them in the centre is a folly in the Rococo sense; its mirrored walls render visible a world of illusion, in which puppets might revolve to the sound of music. There is nothing in this piece resembling a classical structure. In its decoration, however, the formal repertoire of the Empire style plays the dominant part—columns with Ionic or Egyptian capitals, cornices supported by consoles, cyma, pearl and egg-and-dart mouldings, bronze mounts and winged genii with victory wreaths.

A magnificent secretaire, elaborately articulated and decorated with numerous mounts, executed to Schinkel's design demonstrates how close this architect was to the Biedermeier style (Plate 80); for all its pilasters, capitals, and cornices, the piece is not

[1] W. Stengel, *Alte Wohnkultur in Berlin und in der Mark*, Berlin, 1958, p. 62, and plate 46. Thielemann was later given the title 'akademischer Künstler'; he died in 1821.

C. SECRETAIRE, Flensburg, about 1815 to 1820
Walnut and birch root veneer, with bronze mounts. H. 217, W. 104, D. 48.5
From a family collection in Flensburg
Städtisches Museum, Flensburg, inv. no. 16035. See p. 75

D. Linen Cupboard, Hamburg, about 1815
Veneered with birch, with painted decoration. H. 204.5, W. 105, D. 46.5
Museum für Kunst und Gewerbe, Hamburg, inv. no. 1911, 102. See p. 74

architecturally conceived. It is wholly based on the demands of the craftsman and his basic means of expression, the plank.

Some more modest productions must be mentioned alongside these court commissions. In about 1830 a simple display cabinet (Plate 81) was executed to a design by Schinkel by Karl Georg Wanschaff, born in 1775 in Frellstedt, near Helmstedt; his years of travel as a journeyman took him to Hamburg and Berlin where in 1806 he established himself as a cabinet-maker.[1] In the judgement of his contemporaries he was one of the most important and skilled cabinet-makers in Berlin which, at that date, had no lack of exceptionally gifted cabinet-makers. Some statistics compiled in 1831 present the following development; in 1786 there were 617 master-craftsmen and journeymen in the cabinet-making and chair-manufacturing trades; in 1806 there were 1,232; by 1816 there were 1,309 and at the end of the Biedermeier period, in 1830, 2,244 cabinet-makers are recorded in a total population of something over 200,000 citizens.[2] Furniture made in Berlin was celebrated for its elegance, and the quality of its craftsmanship; in 1829 almost twice as much furniture was exported as was imported.[3]

Wanschaff, much assisted by Schinkel, received numerous commissions from the court. In 1816 he furnished Prince August's library, and made furniture for Prince Friedrich's apartments. In 1825 he fitted up the Sommerhaus in Charlottenburg Park, and the apartments of the Crown Prince in the Schloss. In 1829 he was appointed a cabinet-maker to the court, and, in the same year, became a member of the society for the encouragement of Prussian industry, which had been founded in 1820. He did not confine himself to court commissions, but he also made the furnishings of a hunting-castle for the Duke of Radziwill, near Posen, for example, in 1816, and, in 1839, a large bench for a semicircular apse to Schinkel's design for the Duchess of Sutherland in London.

He often manufactured simplified versions of the furniture executed for his aristocratic clients in quantity for his warehouse. He directed his business in partnership with his brother, Bernhard and, from the 1830s onwards, with his son, Julius; he died in 1848.

---

[1] Sievers, op. cit., p. 47ff.

[2] *Zeitblatt für Gewerbetreibende und Freunde der Gewerbe,* Berlin, IV, 1831, p. 193.

[3] C. W. Ferber, *Neue Beiträge zur Kenntniss des gewerblichen und commerciellen Zustandes der Preussischen Monarchie,* Berlin, 1832, p. 48.

The generosity of the display cabinet's proportions, and the delicacy of its mouldings are a tribute to his ability, and to that of its artistic begetter. Also from his workshop, and probably from a design by Schinkel too, is a mahogany sofa decorated with fine maple inlaid stringing lines (Plate 82); it is one of the most elegant and distinguished pieces of seat furniture to have been produced in North Germany.

The strength of Schinkel's affinity with the Biedermeier style is illustrated by an arm-chair which he designed in about 1824 for his most important employer, his royal patron Friedrich Wilhelm III (Plate 83). A further two similar arm-chairs were supplied to the court but the name of the cabinet-maker who executed them is unknown; the way their forms gently curve into one another is a Biedermeier characteristic, as is the openly-revealed construction of the curves of legs and seat, with an accented joint, and a wedge for stability.

Comparison of the sofa executed to his design (Plate 82) with a very similar piece from Schloss Charlottenhof, which was probably made only a little later (Plate 84), provides a demonstration of Schinkel's artistic supremacy; for all the delicacy of its details the latter is, in the last analysis, nothing but the translation of an English proto-type into a middle-class, comfortable piece of furniture.

The strength of the influence of the middle-class Biedermeier style at court is demon-strated by a chair also from Charlottenhof whose modesty of form almost defies further simplification (Plate 85).

In addition to Wanschaff, Schinkel entrusted the execution of his furniture to Johann Christian Sewening, a court cabinet-maker, who carried out numerous commissions for the palaces of the princes between 1816 and 1832. As well as this furniture, he made a number of luxurious pieces inlaid with mother-of-pearl and ivory that he showed at exhibitions. They included a card-table (shown in 1822) and a magnificent table with inlaid decoration (shown in 1830) which commemorated the birthday of the Empress of Russia.

In addition to the numerous cabinet-makers who exhibited at the frequent exhibitions and supplied the court—Böge, J. W. Bidtel, Gottlieb and David Hamann, Ziedrich and many others—and the two furniture factories, directed by C. G. Hörich and Lindemann, the name of one last cabinet-maker must be mentioned, as an exceptionally elegant piece by him survives. The cabinet-maker in question is Adolph Friedrich Voigt who, from 1810 to 1826, showed repeatedly at the Akademie exhibitions. In 1811 an elegant secretaire in the Empire style by Voigt was illustrated in Rockstroh's Journal;[1] however, he used purely Biedermeier forms in a charming secretaire shaped like a fire-screen (Plates 86 and 87). It is signed 'Patent Sekretär Adolph Friedrich Voigt in Berlin Leipziger Strasse Nr. 98' on a small enamel tablet and a signed drawing for the piece, with directions for its construction, also survives. Voigt was strongly influenced by a Sheraton design, Plate XVII in his *Cabinet-Maker and Upholsterer's Drawing-Book* (Plate III), of which an executed example with certain variations survives.[2] This type of furniture was also known during the Empire period, but it was most popular during the Biedermeier period and the early years of historicism. Schinkel also designed a piece of this type,[3] as did La Mésangère, the prolific French designer of the first third of the century.[4] Numerous examples are known, whether through their survival, their description in exhibition reports, or their publication in pattern-books of the period.

It was a type of furniture that possessed all the virtues most prized during the Biedermeier period; it took up little room, was easily moved and, most important of all, was very versatile, being usable for writing, reading, dressing or sewing—and even possibly as a fire-screen. Furthermore it supplied the cabinet-maker with an opportunity to show off his skill; its fall-front was made to fold downwards with all its pigeon-holes, its writing surface could be set in a sloping position to serve as a reading stand, but could also be opened backwards, and the mirror was reversible. Thus an English furniture design of the late eighteenth century was transmuted into one of the most characteristic pieces of Biedermeier furniture.

CENTRAL GERMANY

Like Vienna, Berlin was the capital of a large united country, and, as Viennese furniture had spread through Austria, pieces in the Berlin version of the Biedermeier style

[1] *Journal für Kunst und Kunstsachen, Künsteleien und Mode*, ed. H. Rockstroh, Berlin and Leipzig, II, 1811, p. 314.

[2] Fastnedge, op. cit., plate 83.

[3] Sievers, op. cit., plate 162.

[4] Pierre Antoine Ledoux de la Mésangère, 'Collection des Meubles et d'Objets de Gout', published from 1802 to 1835 as supplements to the *Journal des Dames et des Modes*, No. 708, 1831.

streamed out into Germany. However, in the area between the North German coastal region and the South, which had such a strong stylistic identity, an area roughly outlined by the cities of Cologne, Hanover, Dresden and Kassel, a large variety of influences were at work; extremes met and regional styles were intermingled. Wandering journeymen picked up their style here and there, and considerable influence was exercised by furniture imported from the main centres of the cabinet trade.

Hanover was really part of North Germany and was, therefore, fully within the sphere of influence of the coastal region. A commode from the Hanoverian royal collection exhibits all the characteristics of North German Biedermeier furniture (Plate 88); the combination of its gently curved front, similar to that of a piece from Lübeck (Plate 63), and its simple but well proportioned general shape, give it an air of dignified distinction, and its double top recalls that typical Northern trick of making the top look as if it had been pushed through the basic cube of the piece.

A work-table with a hemispherical body (Plate 89) also exhibits all the characteristics of the North German Biedermeier style, as does the guild chest of the cobblers of Celle, with its variously shaped sunk panels and double top (Plate 90). The latter piece displays special stylistic peculiarities in its choice of woods, its inlaid decoration and, especially, in its concave curved base, although it should be born in mind that guild chests had a traditional shape of their own.

However, the extent of Southern influences on the North is demonstrated by a secretaire in the Kestner Museum in Hanover (Plate 91), which has been strongly influenced by another secretaire in the Museum für angewandte Kunst in Vienna (Plate II). In fact the cabinet-maker who produced the Biedermeier piece (the reasons why it must be Biedermeier have been given on page 48) must have been familiar with the piece in Vienna. For this reason Feulner stated that the secretaire was made in Vienna.[1] But the Viennese Biedermeier style had such a strong character of its own, Viennese cabinet-makers created such original furniture, and the reaction against the Empire style was so strong in Vienna, that it is inconceivable such a piece could have been produced there. Its use of the arched sunk panel typical of North Germany, its employment of a scallop motif—completely unknown in South Germany—in the inlaid decoration of its top section, and its use of mahogany, all point in this direction. Thus a splendid

[1] Feulner, op. cit., 3rd ed., p. 745.

84

example of Viennese Empire furniture has been transformed into a reticent but elegant North German piece, and it is extremely probable that the secretaire was made in Hanover. It must, however, remain an open question whether this reinterpretation of a Viennese piece is the result of a whim on the part of the individual who commissioned it, or of a journeyman's travels, or the production of a craftsman who had come from Vienna.

An example of the great distances which were often travelled by cabinet-makers at this period is provided by Johann Friedrich Schinn, a Celle cabinet-maker, who served his apprenticeship in Mitau in Latvia, later worked in Memel and Leipzig, and finally settled in Celle in 1801.[1] Another example is Christian Härder, a pupil of Roentgen at Neuwied, who moved to Brunswick. It is self-evident that the style of their birth-places, together with everything they had learnt or seen on their travels, accompanied these cabinet-makers to their new homes and places of work.

In the Rhineland cities the influence of the South was stronger and shapes were less austere; this is clearly illustrated by a secretaire in Düsseldorf (Plate 92). Its frontal articulation is less rigorous, and not as carefully conceived, while the semi-circular upper section, whose curved supports carry the rectangular pedimented top, lends the whole piece a somewhat playful air; its use of a light and brilliantly figured birch veneer is also a reflection of Southern fashions.

The Southern delight in comic effects is again apparent in the use of dolphins for table legs, or chair backs or arm-rests, which was very popular in the Rhineland (Plates 93–96). A table (Plate 93) and a sofa (Plate 96) are particularly good examples of the intermixture of Southern delight in elaborate shapes with Northern reticence; both pieces are of mahogany. The typically North German elongated fan ornament below the apron of the sofa appears to extend into the feet, which are applied to the front; the dolphins in the arm-rests are curled up into geometrically exact circles.

Another instance of a combination of the most diverse elements is provided by a birch-wood chair produced in the Rhineland; its crescent-shaped back is supported by two small ebonized columns, themselves supported by sturdy curved legs (Plate 97).

On the other hand, the composer Louis Spohr's secretaire, made by a cabinet-maker

[1] This information has been brought to light through the researches of Dr J. Leister of the Bomann Museum, Celle.

from Kassel in 1822, exhibits those clean, simple forms, characteristic of the Biedermeier style at its purest, such as Danhauser sometimes produced in Vienna; no part of it appears superfluous, and its only decoration is two small applied pilasters and two pediments stressed by mouldings (Plate 99).

An exceptionally graceful round table, executed in Kassel in 1831, was in Schloss Altenstein in Thuringia; it had a vase-shaped central column, from which emerged four widely projecting curved supports for the top.[1]

The masterpiece of Bernhard Stedefeld, a Marburg cabinet-maker, produced in 1819, provides a further example of a mixture of Southern and Northern elements (Plate 100); it incorporates extremely original decorative volutes, reminiscent of an Ionic capital, which curve straight up into the top section, and two arched sunk panels in this section are surmounted by a large inlaid pendant flower; a scallop motif is inlaid in its richly furnished interior.

A secretaire that was probably produced in neighbouring Thuringia, carries the lyre form introduced from Vienna almost to excess (Plate 101); it was executed by a cabinet-maker named Hans Brandt in 1822. Its lateral volutes, connected to one another by a large curved moulding, contain drawers, and its rectangular body looks as if it has been pushed through the curved top section. In 1829 Ludwig Beissner executed an almost literal repetition of this piece, although with a slightly richer interior, as his masterpiece (Plate 102).

A secretaire with a semi-circular top section, probably also made in Thuringia, again reflects the appeal of a striking shape, but its generally restrained arrangement displays North German refinement, while the influence of the Louis XVI style is apparent in its tapered legs, and framed panels (Plate 103). The conception of furniture as a combination of geometric shapes is displayed in a particularly imaginative manner in its upper section, which incorporates a massive arch transfixed by two rectangular blocks, one corresponding to the total width of the piece, and the other to the width of the central door.

In contrast, a secretaire with a totally different formal arrangement, executed as his masterpiece by a cabinet-maker named Liende in 1821, displays remarkable classical tendencies (Plate 104); in it the combination of simple geometric shapes has produced

[1] Bau- und Kunstdenkmäler Thüringens, XXXV, Herzogtum Sachsen-Meiningen, Jena, 1909, p. 36.

an architectural, or rather monumental, solution of exceptional elegance. This piece was certainly made in Dresden, and represents a highly successful combination of the imaginative use of forms peculiar to Vienna, and the classical architectural austerity typical of furniture made in Berlin.

However, it must be stressed that these are isolated and exceptional pieces; the large mass of furniture made in Saxony can scarcely be distinguished from the general run of furniture made elsewhere. From 1824 exhibitions of industry were regularly held in Dresden, and the report on the 1831 exhibition bemoaned the fact that Dresden cabinet-makers 'had by no means equalled the high standard of the great cities of Germany, Vienna, Berlin, and Hamburg'.[1] Nevertheless, a secretaire by a cabinet-maker named Feldmann, and a '*Säulentisch zum Ausziehen*' (a pull-out table with columnar legs) by J. G. B. Beeger, were praised. The influence of Vienna on furniture produced in Saxony, which is still apparent, was indubitably furthered by the exhibitions of Austrian products that took place in Leipzig in 1816 and 1828.[2]

[1] *Bericht über dis Ausstellung sächsischer Gewerb-Erzeugnisse im Jahre 1831*, Dresden and Leipzig, 1832.
[2] *Mittheilungen für Gewerbe und Handel,* published by the Verein zur Ermunterung des Gewerbegeistes in Böhmen, Prague, II, 1836, p. 216.

FIVE

Upholstery

It is difficult now to comprehend the importance of the role played by upholstery during the Biedermeier period. As a result of the impermanence of its materials, and the continual striving to keep rooms and furniture in the latest fashion, the original stuffs have been the subject of wholesale destruction.

Curtains were always artistically draped; the fact that furniture pattern-books also invariably contained illustrations of draped curtains demonstrates the importance attributed to this aspect of interior decoration (Plate 105). A contemporary source stated that 'upholstered sofas and beautifully pleated window curtains are essential elements in a properly furnished house'. In Berlin it was Schinkel who contrived 'to improve taste in upholstery'.[1] Curtain materials were skilfully arranged in folds, and furled over the rods in full drapes, often asymmetrically; their sides were long, and ended in staggered folds, arranged in layers. Transparent blinds that let in the light, and could be seen through, although opaque to someone outside, were hung immediately in front of the windows. However, they also formed a background, which isolated the room from the outside world, and produced a feeling of security in its occupants.

The ideal for the well-furnished living-room of the prosperous citizen remained, as before, to hang its walls with fabric. Wall-papers, which were becoming more and more popular, made use of fabric patterns; there were, in fact, wall-papers printed with *trompe-l'œil* draped fabrics and gathered blinds with pelmets, tassels and fringes.

What was fashionable for rooms was fashionable for furniture. The sofa gave the upholsterer the opportunity of displaying his skill to its best advantage; almost every sofa had cylindrical cushions at each side, and they were an inevitable feature of those whose arm-rests widened at the top in trumpet fashion (Plates 70 and 76).[2] In

[1] *Gemeinnützige Preussische Handels- und Gewerbs-Zeitung*, I, 1838, p. 269.
[2] The upholstery of the sofa in Plate 76 has been wrongly altered at a later date.

some sofas cabinet-work took second place to upholstery (Plate 2), and in extreme cases it was completely displaced so that no wood was visible on the outside of the piece.

The level of artistry achieved by upholstery even when there were no cushions present is illustrated by a sofa designed by the Viennese upholsterer, Lechner (Plate 105); in its upholstered back a patterned fabric alternates with folded drapes of plain stuff, which also hang down over the arm-rests at each side, where they are tied in knots. A design for a chair by Danhauser of Vienna, displays similar hanging drapes of fabric; in it a casual and impermanent arrangement is simulated with the most consummate artistry (Plate 106). Attempts were made to shut off the space underneath seat furniture and thus conceal this area of darkness, most generally in sofas, in which this space was usually more or less completely masked by draperies (Plate 107). Danhauser also executed some designs with this feature,[1] and some chairs have kept such draperies into this century.[2]

The four-poster of course remained in favour as a type of bed. But its popularity was not so much the result of a desire for security or a sign of ostentation; it rather reflected the necessity of isolating and concealing the bed in the living-room, where it was often placed. It is probably for the same reason that every bed had a so-called 'Couvertrahmen', a wooden framework already familiar on the magnificent beds of the Baroque period. These frames, which were put over the bed and its bed-clothes during the day, were fitted out by upholsterers with great imagination during the Biedermeier period. A design by Danhauser must once again serve as an example (Plate 108).

A final mention must be made of work-tables; underneath these was often a large container for materials, which gave the upholsterer yet another opportunity to display his fertility of invention.

Thus during the Biedermeier period upholstery enjoyed a golden age; in fact the founders of the great furniture firms were frequently upholsterers.

Sprung upholstery was another Biedermeier invention; in 1822 Georg Junigl, a Viennese upholsterer, received a patent 'for his improvement on contemporary methods

---

[1] Vienna, Österreichisches Museum für angewandte Kunst, sheet XVI/319.
[2] Ferdinand Luthmer and Robert Schmidt, *Empire und Biedermeiermöbel aus Schlössern und Bürgerhäusern*, Frankfurt, 1923, plates 96f.

of furniture upholstery, which, by means of a special preparation of hemp, and with the assistance of iron springs, he renders so elastic that it is not inferior to horsehair upholstery'.[1]

[1] *Jahrbücher des k.k. polytechnischen Instituts in Wien*, IV, 1823, p. 91. In 1825 Samuel Pratt was awarded a similar patent in London.

SIX

Craftsmanship
in Biedermeier Furniture

In the Biedermeier period there was no change in the principles and regulations relating to the education of the young cabinet-maker established in earlier periods. Apprenticeships generally lasted three years, but sometimes even four, as for example in Vienna, in cases where the apprentice was supplied with clothes by his master; in any case he lodged and boarded with his master's family. When he had passed his examination, the 'journeyman' set out on his travels in order to perfect his expertise.

After a few years of work he could take the examination to qualify as a master-craftsman. Indeed, after the abolition of the guilds' restrictive powers, it could be taken by any citizen of the country .With the introduction of freedom to trade it also ceased to be a prerequisite for the foundation of a workshop—in fact the managers of the larger businesses were often sculptors, gilders or upholsterers. However, it remained, as before, a proof of genuine skill, and was a condition of the right to keep apprentices.[1] The masterpiece (usually a secretaire, but sometimes a commode or a dressing-table, in all cases veneered) had to be designed, costed and executed in four weeks by the journeyman himself.

Great attention was also paid to the further education of master-craftsmen; in nearly every city polytechnics were founded, which concerned themselves with all the problems of the craftsman. At their sessions new inventions were discussed; the products of members exhibited and criticized; machines, tools and materials tested; and foreign products examined. Courses were given in draughtsmanship, and nearly every such institution published its own journal. The journals of other associations, including foreign ones, were subscribed to, and the pattern-books, which were being published everywhere, were made available for inspection.

[1] The revision of the rules affecting the rights of master-craftsmen, and the whole question of freedom to trade, were the subjects of intensive discussion. See Appendix, p. 100.

Life in the master-craftsman's home and workshop had a fixed pattern; all his journeymen, so long as they were unmarried, and his apprentices lodged in his house, and took their meals with him and his wife. Even large businesses, such as the firm of Knussmann in Mainz, which employed up to a hundred people, kept up this custom until the end of the Biedermeier period.

The high degree of competition between the large number of cabinet-makers that resulted from the abolition of guild-imposed restrictions, and the growth of imports, placed severe burdens on the individual craftsman. Nonetheless many of them achieved a considerable level of prosperity; the master-craftsman was usually able to buy or build his own house a relatively short time after setting up his own workshop. The foundation of a number of large enterprises and furniture warehouses proves the existence of a sound commercial basis.

Since the foundation of their craft, little basic change had taken place in cabinet-makers' tools; in the Biedermeier period, saw, plane and chisel remained their basic equipment. However, a whole series of improvements were introduced from England. In 1822 news of the glass-paper used there for polishing furniture was announced for the first time in Germany. In 1825 reports were published on the hand-saw used in England, the so-called 'fox-tail' saw, which Bennington Gill of Birmingham improved in 1823 by the addition of a metal spine. The plane was improved by Williamson and Gladwell, and an adjustable clamp that improved the efficiency of the saw was introduced from England, as was a new tool for setting it. In Berlin in 1830 a German, named Schreiber, was awarded a patent for his double-plane blade.[1]

The machines for woodworking, which were nearly all invented during the period treated here, were of great importance for the future, but were not introduced into a significant number of workshops until the second third of the century. This was symptomatic of the Biedermeier period: it was full of innovation and upheaval but, in the last analysis, still dominated by hand craftsmanship.

---

[1] *Polytechnisches Journal*, edited by J. G. Dingler, Stuttgart, IX, 1822, p. 123; *Jahrbücher des k.k. polytechnischen Instituts in Wien*, VIII, 1826, p. 241; X, 1827, p. 172; XI, 1827, p. 315; XIV, 1829, p. 30; G. Altmütter, *Beschreibung der Werkzeug-Sammlung des k.k. polytechnischen Instituts*, Vienna, 1825, p. 196; *Der Handwerker und Künstler Fortschritte und Muster*, I, 1826, p. 19; and *Gemeinützige Preussische Handels- und Gewerbs-Zeitung*, II, 1834, p. 83.

In 1817 Martin and Aloys Munding of Vienna were awarded a patent for a '*Zirkular-Schneidemaschine*', in other words a circular saw, another machine which was already familiar in England at this period and which was at first used only for cutting veneers. In 1818, a circular saw was imported from England by a Munich businessman named Stöber, and connected to a water-driven hemp mill belonging to a rope manufacturer named Mais. As early as 1821 Aloys Munding was awarded a new patent for his invention of a method of cutting, rather than sawing, veneers. In 1824 Carl Hummel, another Viennese, received a patent for his moulding plane, which again followed English prototypes.[1] In his *Einleitung in die mechanischen Lehren der Technologie*, published in Vienna in 1825, Karl Karmarsch listed four different veneer-cutting machines: the saw, the circular saw, the knife and the plane. He also reported on a cutting-out saw for the execution of inlaid decoration, although he had only heard of it from France, on two different types of planing machine, and on English drilling and mortising machines. In the years 1826 to 1828, however, the following newly invented machines were patented in Bavaria alone—a machine for cutting mouldings, an improved circular saw, a polishing machine and a drilling machine.[2] But as late as 1828 the *Zeitblatt für Gewerbetreibende und Freunde der Gewerbe*, published by Heinrich Weber in Berlin, stated that, 'our establishments for processing timber for building and cabinet-making can scarcely be compared to those existing in France and England. For the moment they are confined to a few, which merely cut building timber and veneers. As yet we have none which execute cabinet-work by machinery.'

Great attention was paid to the manufacture of veneers, and, in particular, to the technique of cutting them by a peeling process, which made it possible to produce un-limited widths. A report of 1817 that a piano-maker named Everyear[3] in St. Petersburg was producing 'sheets of veneer of about a hundred feet in length, and four, five, or even more in width', was countered by the statement that the cabinet-makers of Fürth had already been producing peeled veneer of this type 'for a long period', if in

---

[1] *Jahrbücher des k.k. polytechnischen Instituts in Wien*, I, 1819, p. 403; III, 1822, p. 498; *Kunst- und Gewerbe-Blatt für das Königreich Bayern*, 1818, col. 639; and Keess and Blumenbach, op, cit., p. 738.

[2] *Kunst- und Gewerbe-Blatt*, published by the Polytechnischer Verein für das Königreich Bayern, XV, 1829, col. 325.

[3] Also Ewarpear or Faveryer.

significantly smaller sizes. Completely unseasoned sappy wood or wood that had been soaked in water was used, and peeled veneer of this type was especially popular for curved objects.[1] In 1822 the Viennese Polytechnic Institute produced a prototype of a machine for cutting veneer by the peeling process.[2]

As a consequence of the large unbroken surfaces favoured in Biedermeier furniture, there was much deliberation on the problem of how to protect wood from the results of warping, twisting and splitting. In 1825, news arrived of a process invented by James Falconer Atlee, an Englishman, which involved squeezing the wood through rollers that moved progressively closer to one another, in order to extract the sap.[3] A method of drying wood by steam, on which numerous journals reported in 1826, was also introduced from England.[4] Patents for wood-drying processes were awarded in 1827 to Friedrich Lafite and Franz Weber in Grätz, and in 1828 to Leonhard Glink in Munich.[5]

A completely new method of enriching the appearance of wood, that was first developed during the Biedermeier period, was the art of staining. Hitherto an alteration in the colour of wood had been carried out only to a small extent with inlays, which were nearly always stained green; wood was also soaked in linseed oil to bring out its natural colour, and there was, of course, the immemorial device of colouring wood black to resemble ebony. At the Biedermeier period, however, an increasing number of recipes for giving wood every conceivable colour were published in the journals, and it comes as no surprise to find that methods of imitating mahogany, which were so expensive, played a major role among them.

As with stains, cabinet-makers produced their own polishes, and the journals also supplied numerous recipes for these; their base was usually shellac, but wax, resin, copal and gum arabic were also used. In 1824 it was suggested that some firms should

---

[1] *Wöchentlicher Anzeiger für Kunst- und Gewerbe-Fleiss im Königreich Bayern*, III, 1817, cols. 537ff. and col. 597.

[2] *Jahrbücher des k.k. polytechnischen Instituts in Wien*, III, 1822, p.309ff.

[3] *Neues Kunst- und Gewerbeblatt,* published by the Polytechnischer Verein für das Königreich Baiern, XI, 1825, p. 278, and *Jahrbücher des k.k polytechnischen Instituts in Wien*, X, 1827, p. 121.

[4] *Kunst- und Gewerbeblatt Baiern*, XII, 1826, col. 619, and *Der Handwerker und Künstler Fortschritte und Muster*, I, 1826, col. 159.

[5] Keess and Blumenbach, op. cit., I, p. 737, and *Kunst- und Gewerbeblatt Baiern*, XVIII, 1832, cols. 618ff.

specialize in producing polishes in order to spare cabinet-makers this labour, but this did not come about.[1]

Equally great attention was paid to the production of glue and, in 1823, the process for manufacturing glue from bones was introduced into Germany.[2] Numerous attempts were also made to produce waterproof glue.

These attempts at innovation and the introduction of new methods in every area of craftsmanship retained a tentative character. Nevertheless, they gave notice of the beginning of a new era—the industrial age.

[1] *Neues Kunst- und Gewerbeblatt Baiern*, X, 1824, p. 248.
[2] *Neues Kunst- und Gewerbeblatt Baiern*, IX, 1823, col. 298.

SEVEN

The Aftermath

In the 1830s an anti-classical reaction to the Biedermeier style resulted in the re-adoption of the styles that preceded neo-classicism, in other words in historicism, which was to treat Gothic and Rococo, and Renaissance and Baroque as being of equal validity. Naturally many cabinet-makers continued to produce Biedermeier furniture during this period, but the elaborate forms and structural complexity of other styles, especially the revived Rococo, were not without influence on their products. What had been austere and pure was now filled with uninhibited movement and luxuriant decoration; the tense curves of the true Biedermeier style were transformed into heavy scrolled volutes, flat surfaces were subdivided and broken up, and functionalism sacrificed to appearance. Turned elements were a popular form of ornament, carved decorative features became prominent, and considered, static forms gave way to more daring and reckless constructions.

Ferdinand V of Hungary's secretaire, which was made in Vienna between 1830 and 1835, is a characteristic example of this degeneration of the Biedermeier style (Plate 109); it retains the lyre shape favoured for this type of furniture during the Biedermeier period, and its individual elements are, without exception, derived from the Biedermeier style, as a comparison with the secretaire in Plate 15 demonstrates—it has a cube-shaped base, an incurved intermediate section below the lyre-shaped main section and a curved top section. However, in it the characteristics of the neo-classical Biedermeier style have been exaggerated to an extreme; its base is very low, its intermediate section is deeply recessed but curves out again, its lyre-shaped section is generously curved and its top section is stepped. The application of two cornucopiae render the lyre almost unrecognizable, and their deep gadrooned decoration determines the overall impact of the piece. Its interior niche is disguised by a battery of columns. The general impression of vivacity and an opulent display of luxury is underlined by the use of brilliantly figured ash-wood.

It is admittedly an exceptional display piece executed for a royal patron. However, the very fact that such an exceptionally luxurious piece was made for the court at this date is symptomatic; a few years earlier there had been no difference between furniture made for the court and ordinary middle-class furniture.

A middle-class desk of this period is illustrated in Plate 110; it was executed by A. Einholzer in 1836, as is established by a drawing in the Österreichisches Museum für angewandte Kunst in Vienna.[1] It provides a further example of the misuse and illogical arrangement of Biedermeier elements; for example, the cylinders flanking its writing surface do not grow organically out of it—appearing rather to be applied to it—and the weight of its side pedestals is taken by two remarkably insecure looking curved forms, which are purely decorative in character, supported on turned vase-shaped feet. Its contrived and artificial character is not the result of virtuoso craftsmanship; it is caused by an excessive stress on purely decorative motifs that has the effect of flouting the basic principles of craftsmanship. Wood and wood-construction are not the basis of its formal arrangement; instead its material has taken second place to formal considerations.

An abundance of elaborate decoration is also a feature of a work-table illustrated in Plate 111; its curved legs have undergone a transformation into elongated volutes, and set on the lower part of its baluster-shaped central column are stays which support its top, although they are not organically connected to it. Every part of this piece is richly decorated with gilt mounts.

The new stylistic tendencies are also reflected in a sofa from Schloss Charlottenhof (Plate 112), especially in its unstable looking turned feet and its vigorously curved arm-rests with applied decoration. An exceptionally strong stress on decoration is apparent, too, in a sofa which was probably produced in Munich (Plate 113); indeed the rather fleshy leaf ornament carved on its arms was originally ebonized.

The stylistic tendency which resulted in the apparent transformation of wood in Rococo furniture into a plastic material, also accounts for the form of the four chairs illustrated in Plate 114. Although they no longer belong to the style, all the individual elements of these exceptionally elegant examples of seat furniture are derived from the Biedermeier style. However, they look more like the work of a carver than a cabinet-maker, and in them the Biedermeier liking for 'bent' forms, which always had an

[1] Sheet XVIII g88, p. 8.

element of tension and consciously emphasized the friability of the material, is given a new interpretation. Their backs are sinuously curved in every possible direction, and their bulbous mouldings look as if they have been modelled without any difficulty from some soft composition. Additional decoration is provided by neat turned spindles, but they do not pretend to hold together the bent back at its narrowest point.

It seems to have been an almost logical progression for Michael Thonet to have set to work at about this time to produce furniture made of wood which really was bent.

Bentwood was not a Thonet invention; it had been familiar from time immemorial, especially for ship-building and wheel-felloes, and as early as 1750 an English engineer, Major Trew, built in Brunswick four steam-driven machines for making wood flexible.[1] However, the Biedermeier period witnessed the first significant increase in interest in this method of processing wood, and in the 1820s there were frequent notices on this subject in the journals. In 1830 Thonet began to experiment with bentwood, his aim from the beginning being the mass-production of seat furniture. He was born in 1796, and in 1819 he set up a cabinet-making workshop in his birth-place, Boppard on the Rhine. In 1842, in response to a summons from Metternich, he went to Vienna where he was given the exclusive right to produce bentwood furniture for the whole Austro-Hungarian Empire. A year later he already had a stock-in-hand of 800 chairs, and his business rapidly developed into a world-wide undertaking, producing chairs on an industrial scale which has never since been repeated.[2]

The formal conception of the earliest chairs and arm-chairs produced by this process remained completely Biedermeier in character (Plate 115). They were executed from relatively thin strips of wood, which were bent in a pattern and glued together at the same time. Even these early chairs were produced in such a way that the stretchers and back rails were interchangeable, or, alternatively, could be replaced by differently shaped parts. These simple means, therefore, provided the basis for a mass-produced piece of furniture that could be made in many different versions. The industrial age in furniture manufacture had begun.

[1] *Wöchentlicher Anzeiger für Kunst- und Gewerbe-Fleiss im Königreich Baiern*, II, 1816, col. 297.
[2] H. Heller, *Michael Thonet, Der Erfinder und Begründer der Bugholzmöbelindustrie*, Brünn, n.d. (about 1925).

Appendix

THE INTRODUCTION OF FREEDOM TO TRADE IN BAVARIA

Extract from J. P. Harl, *Entwurf eines Polizei-Gesetzbuchs* (Scheme for a Police Code), Erlangen, 1822, vol. I (pp. 393ff.)

(Where it was not already established, freedom to trade was introduced in the majority of German states during the Biedermeier period. Harl declared himself in favour of its introduction to Bavaria. His penetrating commentary on his legislative proposals is of the greatest interest for an assessment of the economic situation in Germany at the time.)

Freedom to trade must be established as a basic principle. On no account must anyone be forbidden to exercise an honest trade, nor must anyone be granted an exclusive right to such a trade.

The basic and momentous principle of freedom of movement must be established throughout the country.

Every native businessman and artist must be permitted to sell his products or works of art throughout the country, without any limitation to a particular area.

In this way not only is every citizen and inhabitant of the state permitted to order and fetch the goods or products he needs from any native craftsman of his choice, in whatever district or region of the country he may be resident, but the craftsman too is at liberty to deliver these himself to their proprietor or the person who has ordered them, and no less so to finish and install on the spot such products as, because of their nature or function, must be completed in the place they were destined for, or assembled, erected, and connected with other items there for the first time, a category including in particular all products connected with building, especially those of carpenters, masons, painters and cabinet-makers; furthermore he is entitled to do all this without paying any tax whatever to the guilds, of whichever kind these may be, in the district to which the products are brought, or where they are completed.

The following are excepted from guild membership in all circumstances:

(1) *Wholesalers,*

(2) *Carriers,*

(3) *Factory-owners and manufacturers.*

Any limitation *respecting the number of master-craftsmen* may be completely abolished in each and every guild at the discretion of the Government.

Appendix

The present situation of trade swallows up the capital of many beginners in business, encourages unthinking traditionalism, in short has more drawbacks than advantages.

Established privileges must be supplanted by personal rights.

At present the absolute right of a master-craftsman to practise any trade is *de facto* established in some states; just as, in certain states, a master-craftsman may employ an unlimited number of journeymen.

If *freedom to trade* is established, *skilled, energetic and thrifty citizens* will be assured of their livelihood.

If manufacture is made easier, consumption will grow, because products can be produced more cheaply and easily. A skilled craftsman will not go out looking for orders; they will come to him. But if a lazy and undistinguished craftsman lives in grand style, it is not freedom to trade which will ruin him.

If those who wish to acquire the privileges of a master-craftsman are obliged to obey the following rules, and if it is ensured that no master-craftsman, by employing an excessive number of journeymen, can acquire the monopoly of a trade, the right of the master-craftsman to practise his trade can, and should, be made absolute.

The privileges of a master-craftsman consist in the following rights:

(1) to practise his craft or trade on his own account;

(2) to have apprentices;

(3) to have journeymen;

(4) to participate in the privileges of his guild, of whichever kind this may be.

Before the privileges of a master-craftsman are granted, proof must be given of the following:

(1) irreproachable behaviour vouched for by trustworthy testimonials;

(2) the necessary property or capital, from 100 to 1000 fl., or more;

(3) attainment of majority proved by a certificate of baptism or birth;

(4) ability tested by the prescribed examination.

No tradesman may be granted *the privileges of a master-craftsman*, unless he has previously acquired *the rights of citizenship*.

In this way it is made impossible for incompetent and impecunious swindlers to insinuate themselves into the privileges of citizen and master-craftsman, and an unlimited number of master-craftsmen does not become a drawback.

The relationship between master-craftsman and journeyman must also be defined by comprehensive regulations.

If a journeyman starts to work for a certain master-craftsman, he must immediately enter into agreement with him, in particular on the following subjects:

(1) the length of his contract, which depends entirely on the wishes and stipulations of the parties to the contract;

(2) his wages;

(3) his lodgings;

(4) his board, which the journeyman himself can take care of, or the master-craftsman can undertake to provide, with or without a deduction from the agreed wages.

The contract between the journeyman and the master-craftsman will only become binding after a probationary period of fourteen days has passed.

It is the master-craftsman's right and duty to supervise the conduct of his journeymen, to exhort them to moral behaviour and to restrain them, to the limit of his powers, from vice and debauchery.

The journeyman is under an obligation:

(1) to undertake the work he is entrusted with, and perform it well and industriously according to the master-craftsman's instructions;

(2) to treat the master-craftsman with outward respect and be faithful to him, and to conform with his domestic arrangements;

(3) to work strictly and diligently all the hours appointed for work, every workday, in order to earn his stipulated wages.

The police should attend to the general publication of useful inventions and discoveries in the field of trade and the applied arts.

Training schools for future craftsmen and artists are a practical means towards the improvement of trade and the applied arts. The general distribution of better instruments and machinery can also make an important contribution towards this end.

Annual public exhibitions of the most superior works of industry and art, not confined to the capital but also in the regional towns, have already proved their worth in several countries. They encourage artistic industry: they maintain a general, and very advantageous spirit of competition among tradesmen and artists; and they give able master-craftsmen and artists an opportunity to introduce their works to the public.

Prizes or *honourable mentions* should be awarded by the Government for important new inventions and improvements in the field of art industry, or for exemplary masterpieces, and the names of those honoured in this manner should be publicly announced.

By these means can be achieved the improvement of production techniques, all important in its consequences, and their wider application to new products, in fact the expansion and advancement of industry in the strictest sense of the word.

For *industry* is a more efficient application of one's corporal and intellectual powers, combined with an economical use of time. Its immediate, direct aim is the improvement and increase of the products of work by means of an increase in activity and an advance in skill. Industry, which, at its highest level, results in the most complete, efficient and rapid use of one's natural powers, is by no means a mere commonplace activity; indeed it should be preferred to diligence. For diligence is often a somewhat mechanical quality, contented with what is inevitable and conventional; whereas industry is an intellectual quality, which is always making progress, always taking advantage of every new opportunity. It is inventive, always seeking out new objects and bringing them to perfection, in the process trying to economize in time or in effort. The man of industry is a hundred years ahead of the diligent worker, if not a thousand!

The true goal of the momentous alliance of civilization and industry, and the maximum encouragement of both, can be none other than to promote to the utmost the happiness of the individual members of the national whole, achieved by a judicious use of all nature's gifts to man, and, by this encouragement, to bring about at the same time a high degree of national prosperity. The civilization of a country and its national industry are the sources of the well-being of citizens, of wealth of nations, and of the revenues of governments; they are the foundation-stones of the happiness of the people and the power of the state.

Just as industry and civilization increase the individual's prosperity and enjoyment of life, so do they spread contentment and peace among all conditions and classes of people; they give the state inner strength and stability and make it powerful through wealth and increase of population. For industry and civilization have a great and beneficial effect on the birth-rate.

It is in fact a universally valid principle that the birth-rate keeps pace with industry and civilization, so that the inhabitants of a country become more numerous at the same rate as they progress in industry and civilization.

Accordingly in any state the greater and more general the industry of the nation and the civilization of the country the smaller the number of unproductive workers or professional idlers, in the unemployed, the needy and the poor. But the more the number of mere consumers in a nation decreases, and that of productive workers grows, the more its *total annual output* can, and indeed must, grow; on this depends the *net national income* which is of paramount and crucial importance, as far as the prosperity of the people and the finances of the state are concerned. On this latter factor depends the national economic balance, which is expressed by the amount of the annual surplus of total national output over the total of national consumption, and is the vital principle underlying the existence of nations.

If, therefore, the prosperity of the citizens and the well-being of the nation are to be encouraged, if individuals and classes are to be made richer, then civilization and industry must be dominant and make continually greater progress.

This is the sole correct and sure method of ensuring an abundance, and a surplus, of the products of nature and art.

However the accumulation of these commodities will, on the one hand, make it unnecessary to spend money abroad and, on the other, attract foreign money into the country.

An increase in exports of merchandise and a decrease in imports contribute towards making the country's balance of trade favourable, in a general and overall sense at least.

Thus the less natural and manufactured products a country needs to import from abroad, and the more of its raw materials, manufactures and works of art it can export abroad, the more its outward trade will exceed its inward trade, and the greater its *independence in trade* will become, which has the most salutary effect on that important factor, the *rate of exchange*.

A country's legal code has an enormous influence on its civilization, its national industry, the well-being of the state, and the prosperity of its citizens. In states where the statute books are closest to perfection, especially with regard to economics, the wealth of the nation also advances. But impractical laws inhibit national industry, impede a country's civilization, impair annual production and endanger the national economic balance, and also, therefore, the balance of trade.

Legislation can act as a spur to the active instincts of the citizen; it can remove any obstacles from his path, and can formulate means for his encouragement.

The specialized science of jurisprudence seems still to be so backward in Germany, that no one has as yet produced a police code, still less a full code, which contains an equitable and complete set of laws to deal with agriculture, manufacture and trade. With this in mind, how many lacunae, flaws and defects must there exist almost throughout statute law!

It is extremely important and imperatively necessary, especially at our time in history, that all those of the state's laws and public institutions which are generally concerned with the national economy and particularly with agriculture, manufactures and trade, should harmonize with the natural laws of a country's civilization and national industry, and consequently of its national wealth, and that they should have as a goal the prosperity of the national whole through the well-being of the individual. It is in fact of great universal importance that the state's laws and institutions not only should not have an unfavourable influence of any kind on civilization and industry, but that they should also eliminate everything which could obstruct these, and with them the well-being of one and all.

However all measures and regulations which have a detrimental effect, indirectly or directly, on the expansion or improvement of agriculture, manufacture and trade, on the healthy circulation of capital, or on the beneficial increase of population, are in fact directed against civilization and industry, and therefore against the prosperity of the nation, which results from these.

In these present times of money shortage, together with the scarcity of credit, trade and food, whose daily increasing consequences should be a matter for grave concern to any patriotically inclined politician or economist, it seems to me that the immediate establishment of a *national chamber of economy* is a real, universal and pressing necessity for a modern state. This new chamber, of extreme general importance, and thus of great public benefit, would not only have to occupy itself with *general legislation concerning the national economy,* but also with *all individual regulations affecting agriculture, manufactures, industry and trade.* However, it would not confine itself to a mere revision, in general or particular, of the existing legislation concerning the national economy, but should extend its field of activity to new laws affecting the national economy. It should take as its guiding stars the natural laws which are the source of the wealth of the nation, and the experience of all eras and countries in order to seek to the best of its ability to remove all hindrances to the expansion and improvement of the three main branches of the nation's trade, in particular that of *marketing native merchandise at home and abroad.*

Congresses of learned societies, whatever form they took, could not render superfluous this new institution which the needs of the time so imperatively demand, nor replace it, for this reason alone, that the application of their conclusions is arbitrary and random.

Bibliography

T. Clemmensen, *Signerede arbejder af københavnske snedkere, Københavns Snedkerlang gennem fire hundrede år, 1554-1954*, Copenhagen, 1954

W. H. Dammann, *Erste Hälfte des neunzehnten Jahrhunderts*, Kunstformenbibliothek, 2nd series, Godesberg, 1922

Bernward Deneke, ' "Biedermeier" in Mode und Kunsthandwerk 1890-1905', *Anzeiger des Germanischen Nationalmuseums*, 1967, p. 163ff.

Rupert Feuchtmüller and Wilhelm Mrazek, *Biedermeier in Österreich*, Vienna, 1963

Adolf Feulner, *Kunstgeschichte des Möbels*, Berlin, 1927 (3rd ed., 1930)

Hartwig Fischel, 'Louis seize, Empire und Biedermeier, Die bildenden Künste', *Wiener Monatshefte*, II, 1919, p. 273ff.

Hartwig Fischel, 'Möbelentwürfe der Empire- und Biedermeierzeit', *Kunst und Kunsthandwerk*, XXIII, 1920, p. 100ff.

Ernst Fischer, *Svenska möbler i bild*, Stockholm, 1931 and 1950

Josef Folnesics, *Innenräume und Hausrat der Empire- und Biedermeierzeit in Österreich-Ungarn*, Vienna, 1902 (5th ed., 1922)

Friederike Klauner, 'Der Wohnraum im Wiener Biedermeier', doctoral thesis, Vienna, 1941 (MS)

Erik Lassen, *Danske Möbler: den Klassiske Periode*, Copenhagen, 1958

J. H. Lexow, *Bergenske Empiremøbler*, Bergen, 1948

Ferdinand Luthmer, *Deutsche Möbel der Vergangenheit*, Leipzig, 1902

Ferdinand Luthmer, *Bürgerliche Möbel aus dem ersten Drittel des 19. Jahrhunderts*, Frankfurt, 1904 (2nd ed., 1918)

Ferdinand Luthmer and Robert Schmidt, *Empire und Biedermeiermöbel aus Schlössern und Bürgerhäusern*, Frankfurt, 1923

Bibliography

JOSEF AUGUST LUX, *Von der Empire- zur Biedermeierzeit*, Stuttgart, 1906 (7th ed., 1930)

PAUL MEBES, *Um 1800*, Munich, 1908 (3rd ed., 1920)

PETER W. MEISTER and HERMANN JEDDING, *Das schöne Möbel im Lauf der Jahrhunderte*, Heidelberg, 1958

SIGRID MÜLLER-CHRISTENSEN, *Alte Möbel vom Mittelalter bis zum Jugendstil*, Munich, 1948 (7th ed., 1968)

GÜNTER SCHADE, *Deutsche Möbel aus sieben Jahrhunderten*, Leipzig, 1966

A. SCHESTAG, 'Zur Entstehung und Entwicklung des Biedermeierstils', *Kunst und Kunsthandwerk*, VI, 1903, p. 236ff.; VII, 1904, p. 415ff.; IX, 1906, p. 568ff.

ROBERT SCHMIDT, *Möbel*, Berlin, 1913 (9th ed., Brunswick, 1965)

HERMANN SCHMITZ, *Vor hundert Jahren, Festräume und Wohnzimmer des deutschen Klassizismus und Biedermeier*, Berlin, 1920

HERMANN SCHMITZ, *Deutsche Möbel des Klassizismus*, Stuttgart, 1923

HERMANN SCHMITZ, *Das Möbelwerk*, Berlin, 1926

JOHANNES SIEVERS, *Die Möbel, Karl Friedrich Schinkel Lebenswerk*, Berlin, 1950

SIGURD WALLIN, *Nordiska museets möbler . . .*, Stockholm, 1931–35

FRANZ WINDISCH-GRAETZ, 'Le bon gout selon M. Biedermeier', *Connaissance des Arts*, XCI, 1959, p. 76ff.

The Plates

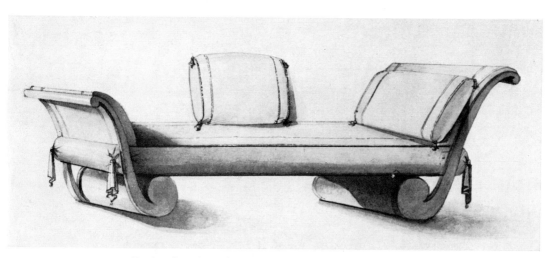

1. Design for a SOFA by JOSEF DANHAUSER, Vienna, about 1820
Pencil and pen wash
Österreichisches Museum für angewandte Kunst, Vienna, sheet XX/415. See p. 55

2. SOFA by JOSEF DANHAUSER, Vienna, about 1820
Formerly in Schloss Laxenburg. *Bundes-Mobilien-Verwaltung, Vienna, inv. no. L 10885.* See pp. 55 and 89

3. Design for a PIER COMMODE, 'Modell Nr. 17, Erzherzog Karl', by JOSEF DANHAUSER, Vienna, about 1815
Pencil and wash
Österreichisches Museum für angewandte Kunst, Vienna, sheet XL/1111. See p. 55

4. PIER COMMODE by JOSEF DANHAUSER, Vienna, about 1815
Deal veneered with mahogany. H. 145.5, W. 95, D. 47
Fürstlich Thurn und Taxis'sches Schloss, Regensburg
A commode *en suite* is in the same collection. See p. 55

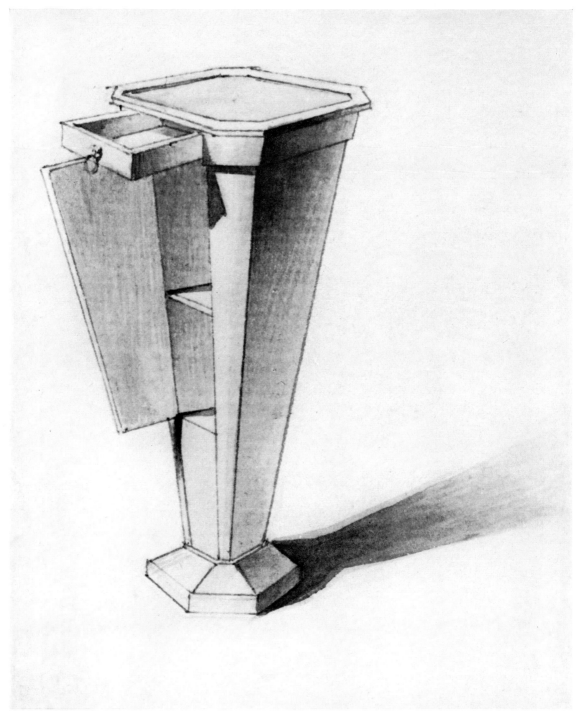

5. Design for a NIGHT TABLE by JOSEF DANHAUSER, Vienna, about 1815 to 1820
Pencil and wash
Österreichisches Museum für angewandte Kunst, Vienna, sheet XLIV/1195. See p. 56

6. NIGHT TABLE by JOSEF DANHAUSER, Vienna, about 1815 to 1820
Mahogany with a marble slab and bronze mounts. H. 83, W. 41.5, D. 39.5
Fürstlich Thurn und Taxis'sches Schloss, Regensburg. See p. 56

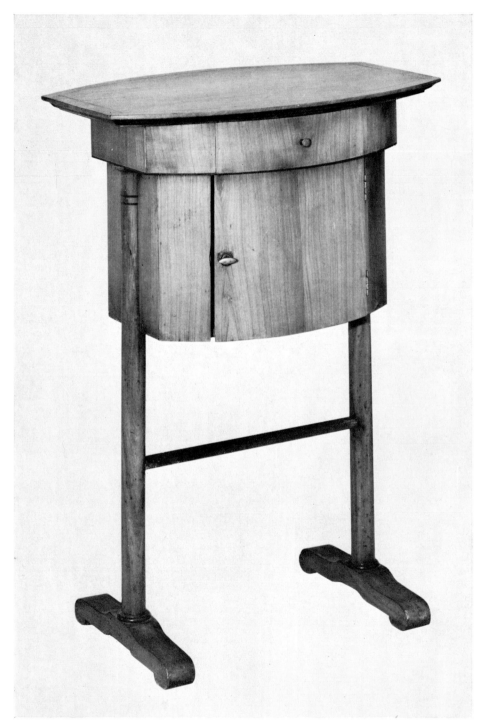

7. NIGHT TABLE by JOSEF DANHAUSER, Vienna, about 1820
Cherrywood. H. 85, W. 60, D. 42
Schloss Heiligenkreuz, near Vienna. See p. 56

8. TABLE by JOSEF DANHAUSER, Vienna, about 1820
Cherrywood. H. 79, W. 127, D. 62
Schloss Heiligenkreuz, near Vienna. See p. 56

9. TABLE, Vienna, about 1820 to 1825
Light walnut. H. 79.5, W. 154, D. 54.5
Fürstlich Thurn und Taxis'sches Schloss, Regensburg. See p. 57

10. TABLE, Vienna, about 1830 to 1835
Burr birch. H. 75, W. & D. 94
Schloss Heiligenkreuz, near Vienna. See p. 57

11. Small LADY'S WRITING DESK by HOLL, Vienna, about 1825

H. 103.5, W. 73, D. 49. *Museum für Kulturgeschichte und Kunstgewerbe, Graz, inv. no. 0 720 (purchased in the Vienna art market)*
Below the centre of one of the pedestals, where the stretchers join, is carved 'A I'. See p. 58

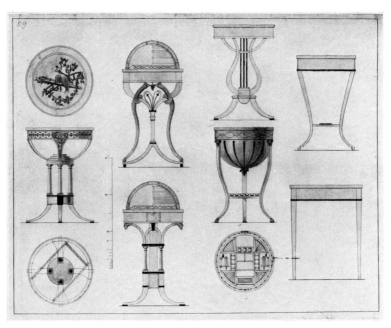

12. STUDENT'S DRAWING executed in Carl Schmidt's drawing school, Vienna, about 1825
Pen and wash
Österreichisches Museum für angewandte Kunst, Vienna, sheet XVIII d III 3. See p. 59

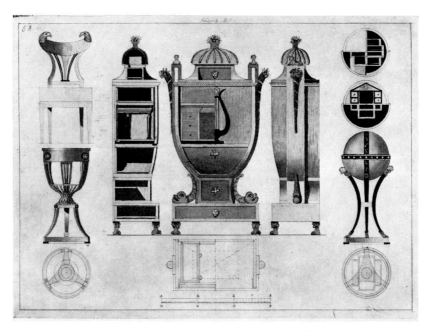

13. STUDENT'S DRAWING by FRIEDRICH PAULICH executed in Carl Schmidt's drawing school, Vienna, about 1825
Pen and wash
Österreichisches Museum für angewandte Kunst, Vienna, sheet XVIII d III 44. See pp. 59, 61

14. GLOBE-SHAPED WORK-TABLE, Vienna, about 1825 to 1830, by a designer in the Carl Schmidt circle
Private collection at Baden, near Vienna
(Feuchtmüller and Mrazek, plate 62; Helena Hayward, *World Furniture*, New York, 1965, p. 259, plate 990). See p. 60

15, 16. Writing Bureau, Vienna, about 1815 to 1820
Deal veneered with mahogany. H. 144, W. 55, D. 41.5
Bayerisches Nationalmuseum, Munich, inv. no. 66/22 (Münchner Jahrbuch der bildenden Kunst, 3rd series, XVIII, 1967, p. 257; Casa d'Oro, II, 1968, p. 659). See pp. 60, 61

17. WRITING BUREAU, Vienna, about 1820

Deal veneered with mahogany, with applied decoration of ebonized pearwood, the interior veneered with rippled maple

H. 168, W. 87, D. 48.5

Museum für Kunsthandwerk, Dresden inv. no. 37507. (G. Messner, 'Zu einigen Möbelneuerwerbungen des Museums für Kunsthandwerk Dresden', *Staatliche Kunstsammlungen Dresden, Jahrbuch 1967*, p. 139)

A very similar example, though somewhat more richly decorated, was formerly in a Viennese private collection (Folnesics, plate 32). See p. 61

18. SMALL TABLE, Vienna, about 1830
Veneered with various burr woods, decorated with inlay in maple. H. 78, W. 78, D. 45
Österreichisches Museum für angewandte Kunst, Vienna, inv. no. H 1039 (Meister and Jedding, plate 543). See p. 61

19. WORKSTAND, its height adjustable, Vienna, about 1820
Mahogany
Bundes-Mobilien-Verwaltung, Vienna, inv. no. Dc 15002
Originally in Franz I's study in the Hofburg in Vienna
The painting let into the top shows Emperor Franz I surrounded by his family. See p. 61

20. TABLE, Vienna, about 1820 to 1825
Burr birch, ebonized pearwood, the lions' paw feet green with bronze collar mounts. H. 83, D. 161
Fürstlich Thurn und Taxis'sches Schloss, Regensburg. See p. 62

21. CONSOLE TABLE with semicircular top, Vienna, about 1820 to 1830
Veneered with mahogany
Formerly in Schloss Laxenburg. *Bundes-Mobilien-Verwaltung, Vienna, inv. no. L 10945*

22. TABLE, Prague, about 1820 to 1830
Cherrywood
Národni Galerie, Prague (J. Durdik and others, *Das grosse Bilderlexikon der Antiquitäten*, Prague, 1968, plate 54). See p. 63

23. CUPBOARD, Hungary, about 1830
Liszt Museum, Sopron. See p. 63

24. WORK-TABLE, Budapest or Vienna, about 1820 to 1830

H. 82

Zagreb Museum. See p. 63

25. BED from Schloss Opeka, probably Zagreb, about 1830
H. 150, W. 110, L. 196
Zagreb Museum. See p. 63

26. CHAIR, Vienna, about 1820 to 1830
Mahogany. H. 80.5, W. 45.5, D. 50
*Österreichisches Museum für angewandt Kunst,
Vienna, inv. no. H 1772 b*

27. SPITTOON, Vienna, about 1820
Veneered with maple
Formerly in the Imperial collection
*Bundes-Mobilien-Verwaltung, Vienna,
inv. no. B 1973*

28. SECRETAIRE, Munich, about 1820
Formerly in the Residenzmuseum, Munich. See p. 66

29. DESK, Munich, about 1815 to 1820, from the Residenz
Stadtmuseum, Munich. See p. 66

30. CUPBOARD, attributed to JOHANN GEORG HILTL, Munich, about 1820
Deal veneered with cherrywood, decorated with transfer prints. H. 200, W. 128.5, D. 50.5
Fürstlich Thurn und Taxis'sches Schloss, Regensburg
Its pendant is in the same collection. See p. 66

31. Secretaire, Munich, about 1820
Walnut, the interior veneered with bird's-eye maple. H. 166, W. 95, D. 46
Stadtmuseum, Munich, inv. no. 35/2178. See p. 66

32. BOOKCASE, Munich, about 1820
Cherrywood. H. 198, W. 131, D. 39
Stadtmuseum, Munich, inv. no. 35/2121. See p. 67

33. TABLE, Munich, about 1820
Cherrywood
Residenzmuseum, Munich. See p. 67

34. CONSOLE TABLE, Munich, about 1820 to 1825
Cherrywood with ebonized beading. H. 87, W. 69, D. 39
Stadtmuseum, Munich, inv. no. 48/102. See p. 67

35. Table, Munich, about 1825 to 1830
Residenzmuseum, Munich. See p. 67

36. CHAIR, Augsburg, about 1820
Cherrywood, with mounts of stamped brass sheet. H. 88.5, W. 35, D. 42
Städtisches Maximilianmuseum, Augsburg. See p. 68

37. CUPBOARD from Regensburg Town Hall, Regensburg, about 1820 to 1830
Cherrywood with ebonized mouldings and astragals in the form of crossed keys. H. 207, W. 164, D. 45
Städtisches Museum, Regensburg. See p. 68

38. COMMODE, Central Franconia, about 1820
Deal veneered with cherrywood, decorated with framing bands of mahogany. H. 88, W. 105, D. 54
Originally made for Eugène Beauharnais, Duke of Leuchtenberg, for his palace in Eichstätt
Later moved to Regensburg and Nuremberg, and finally to the Residenz in Munich
Stadtmuseum, Munich, inv. no. 35/2162
Two commodes with two drawers on tall legs and a pier commode with six drawers belonged *en suite*. See p. 68

39. CUPBOARD, probably Regensburg, about 1820 to 1825
Poplar, with walnut framing bands, a brass gallery, and black composition inlay. H. 207, W. 97, D. 44
Städtisches Museum, Regensburg. See p. 68

40. SECRETAIRE, probably Regensburg, about 1820 to 1825
Walnut, maple, and ebonized pearwood. H. 147, W. 102.5, D. 48
Fürstlich Thurn und Taxis'sches Schloss, Regensburg. See pp. 68, 69

41. SECRETAIRE, Central Franconia, about 1825 to 1830
Mahogany, with an earlier panel of scagliola let into the fall-front. H. 185, W. 107, D. 40
Deutschordensschloss, Ellingen. See pp. 68, 69

42. SOFA with storage space, probably Regensburg, about 1820 to 1825
Walnut decorated with ebonized columns and pediments, and mounts of stamped brass sheet. The covering about 1900
The sides are covered with cloth and can be opened as doors. H. 109, W. 192, D. 74.5
Städtisches Museum, Regensburg. See p. 69

43. BOOKCASE, Franconia, about 1820
Cherrywood. H. 234, W. 188, D. 44
Staatsbibliothek, Bamberg. See p. 69

44. CONSOLE TABLE, Franconia, about 1820
Deal veneered with cherrywood. H. 78.5, W. 96.5, D. 60.5
Kunstsammlungen, Veste Coburg

45. TABLE, Bavaria, about 1825 to 1830
Walnut, the top inlaid with marble. H. 80, D. 83
Stadtmuseum, Munich, inv. no. 30/1883

46. SMALL TABLE, probably Regensburg, about 1820 to
1830. Mahogany. H. 74.5, W. 73, D. 49
Städtisches Museum, Regensburg

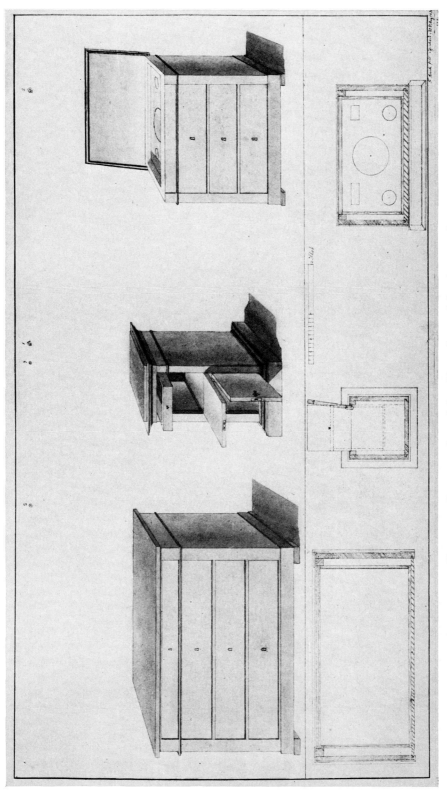

47. DRAWING of a commode, a night table, and a wash-hand commode,
into whose upper section the various washing utensils are fitted
Pen and wash, signed: 'F Storck fecit Offenbach d. 21te Aug. 1830'
Staatliche Kunstbibliothek, Berlin, inv. no. 5367. See p. 71

48. COMMODE, South-West Germany, about 1815 to 1820
Walnut with ebonized columns and mounts of stamped tin
Schloss Meersburg on Lake Constance. See p. 71

49. COMMODE, South-West Germany, about 1825 to 1830
Veneered with walnut, with ebonized columns and mounts of stamped brass sheet
Rosgartenmuseum, Konstanz. See p. 71

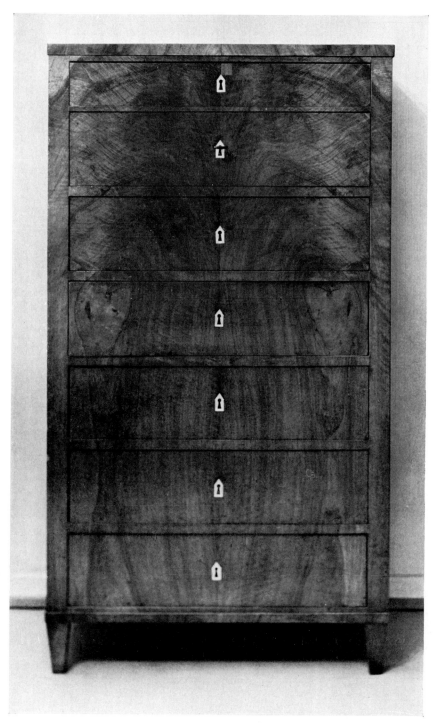

50. PIER COMMODE, South-West Germany, about 1815
Deal veneered with walnut. H. 133, W. 76, D. 40
Private collection, Karlsruhe. See p. 71

51. SECRETAIRE, South-West Germany, about 1820 to 1825
Pearwood. H. 189.5, W. 102, D. 51.5
Historisches Museum der Pfalz, Speyer, inv. no. 1950/124. See p. 71

52. CHAIR, South-West Germany, about 1815 to 1820
Veneered with cherrywood, with black painted
decoration. H. 89, W. 48, D. 41
Schloss Schwetzingen, inv. no. G 1505. See p. 71

53. CHAIR, South-West Germany, about 1815 to 1825
Veneered with cherrywood
Schloss Meersburg on Lake Constance. See p. 71

54. CHAIR, South-West Germany, about 1815 to 1820
Cherrywood. H. 90.5, W. 43.5, D. 42.5
Schloss Schwetzingen, inv. no. G 1234. See p. 71

55. CHAIR, South-West Germany, about 1815
Cherrywood. H. 87.3, W. 48.3, D. 39.5
*Historisches Museum der Pfalz, Speyer,
inv. no. HM 1955/54.* See p. 71

56. SOFA, South-West Germany, about 1825 to 1830
Cherrywood. L. 180
Kunsthaus am Museum, Cologne, Sale number 38 of 1969. See p. 71

57. NEEDLEWORK HOLDER, South-West Germany, about 1815 to 1820
Veneered with yew. H. 76, D. 49
Schloss Schwetzingen, inv. no. G 1345 (*Die Kunstdenkmäler Badens*, X, 2, p. 82). See pp. 72, 73

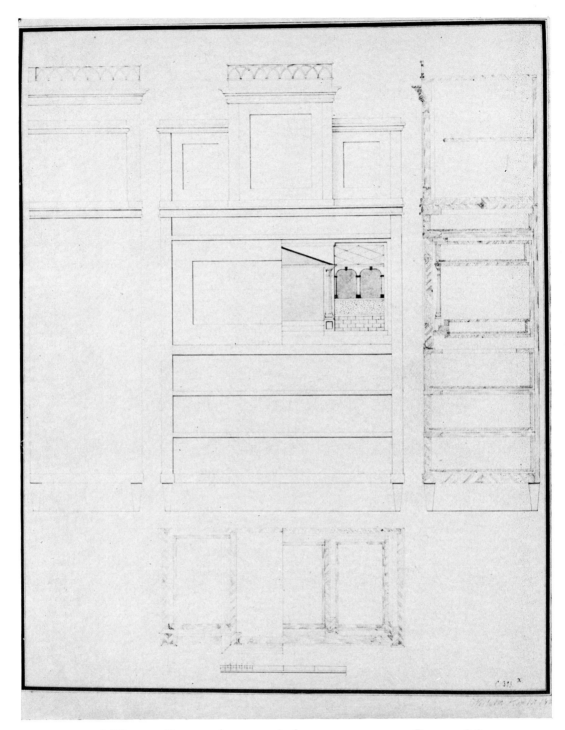

58. WORKING DRAWING for a secretaire by WILHELM HEMCKER, Bremen, 1828
Pen and wash. 38 × 30.5
Focke-Museum, Bremen, inv. no. C 393x. See p. 73

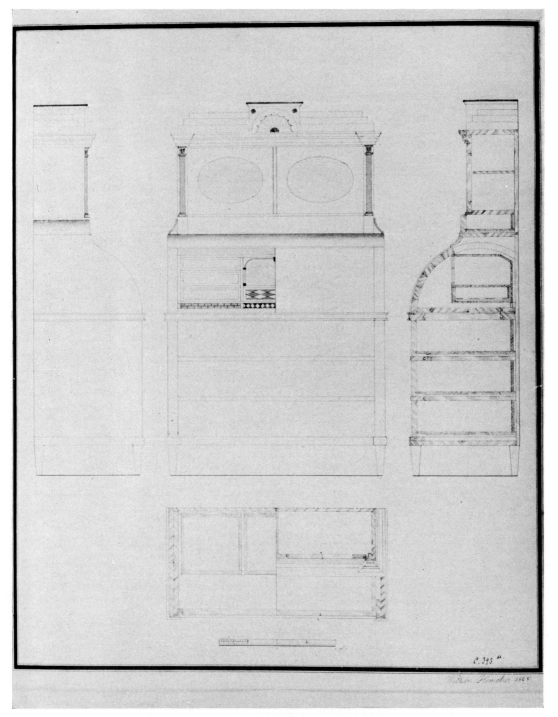

59. WORKING DRAWING for a secretaire by WILHELM HEMCKER, Bremen, 1828
Pen and wash. 39 × 32
Focke-Museum, Bremen, inv. no. C 393n. See p. 73

60. WINE COOLER, Bremen, about 1830
Veneered with walnut. H. 78, D. 49
Focke-Museum, Bremen, inv. no. 0 267. See p. 73

61. BOOKCASE, probably Hamburg, about 1820
Veneered with mahogany, with ivory insets, and bronze mounts. H. 185, W. 106.5, D. 46
Museum für Kunst und Gewerbe, Hamburg. See p. 74

62. CORNER CUPBOARD, Lübeck, about 1815
Oak veneered with mahogany, decorated with ebonized pearwood, and bronze mounts. H. 300
Museen für Kunst und Kulturgeschichte, Lübeck, inv. no. 1927/18 (Lübecker Kunstpflege 1920–1933 Fig. 28). See p. 74

63. COMMODE, Lübeck, about 1820 to 1825
Deal veneered with mahogany, the interior of oak, decorated with bronze mounts. H. 90, W. 100, D. 56
Museen für Kunst und Kulturgeschichte, Lübeck, inv. no. 1910/109. See pp. 75, 84

64. Two CHAIRS, Lübeck *Left*: about 1815 *Right* about 1820 to 1825
Cherrywood, inlaid with maple with pokerwork decoration. H. 85, W. 49, D. 45
Walnut. H. 86, W. 46, D. 46
Museen für Kunst und Kulturgeschichte, Lübeck (Left chair, inv. no. 1905/136). See p. 75

65. COMMODE, Flensburg, about 1815 to 1820

Deal veneered with walnut, with ebonized edges and inset panel at the top, and stamped and cast mounts. H. 81, W. 84, D. 46

Städtisches Museum, Flensburg, inv. no. 16038. See p. 76

66. COMMODE, Flensburg, about 1820 to 1830

Pine veneered with mahogany, with inset panels of birch. H. 82, W. 79.2, D. 44.8

Schleswig-Holsteinisches Landesmuseum, Schleswig. See p. 76

67. SOFA, Holstein, probably about 1820
Veneered with mahogany, with inlaid decoration in maple. H. 89, W. 196.5, D. 75
Schleswig-Holsteinisches Landesmuseum, Schleswig (E. Sauermann, *Alt-Schleswig-Holstein*, Berlin, 1912, plate 136;
Schmitz, *Möbelwerk*, p. 303; Dammann, plate 11). See p. 76

68. WORK TABLE, Kiel, about 1820 to 1825
Veneered with mahogany, inlaid with maple, the strings of the lyre in brass. H. 82, W. 62, D. 49.5
Schleswig-Holsteinisches Landesmuseum, Schleswig, inv. no. 1908/82
(Dammann, plate 18; Schmidt, plate 226; Luthmer and Schmidt, plate 111b). See p. 76

69. TABLE, Kiel, about 1815 to 1820
Veneered with mahogany, with bronze feet. H. 74, D. 116
Schleswig-Holsteinisches Landesmuseum, Schleswig, inv. no. 1921/261. See pp. 51, 76

70. SOFA, Holstein, probably about 1825
Veneered with mahogany, with bronze mounts. H. 93, W. 231, D. 68
Schleswig-Holsteinisches Landesmuseum, Schleswig, inv. no. 1906/172 (E. Sauermann, *Alt-Schleswig-Holstein*, Berlin,
1912, Plate 137; Dammann, plate 11; Luthmer and Schmidt, p. 145; Schmitz, *Deutsche Möbel*, p. 226). See p. 88

71. CHAIR, Holstein, about 1815
Mahogany, inlaid with maple. H. 81, W. 45.5
Schleswig-Holsteinisches Landesmuseum,
Schleswig, inv. no. 1907/219
(Dammann, plate 18; Luthmer and Schmidt,
Plate 111b). See p. 88

72. CHAIR, Holstein, probably about 1820
Cherrywood and birch. H. 89.5, W. 47, D. 41.5
Schleswig-Holsteinisches Landesmuseum,
Schleswig, inv. no. 1923/8

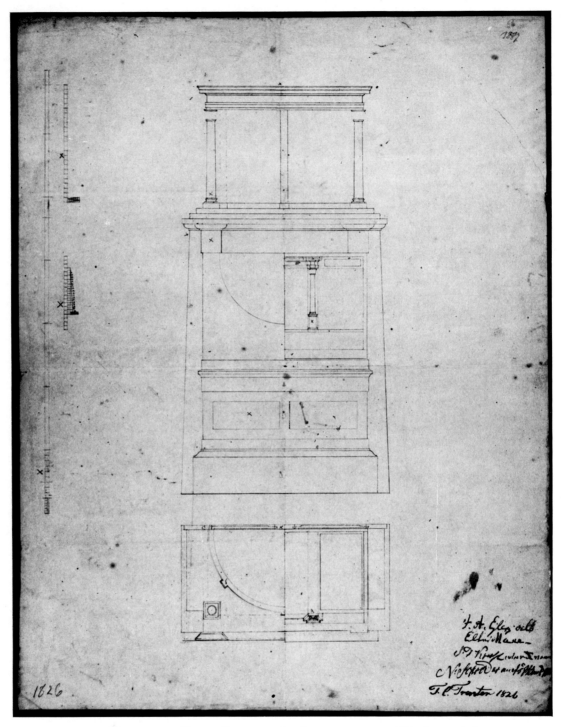

73. MASTERPIECE DESIGN for a secretaire, by F. C. TRENTER, Oldenburg, 1826
Landesmuseum für Kunst- und Kulturgeschichte, Oldenburg, inv. no. 3887. See p. 77

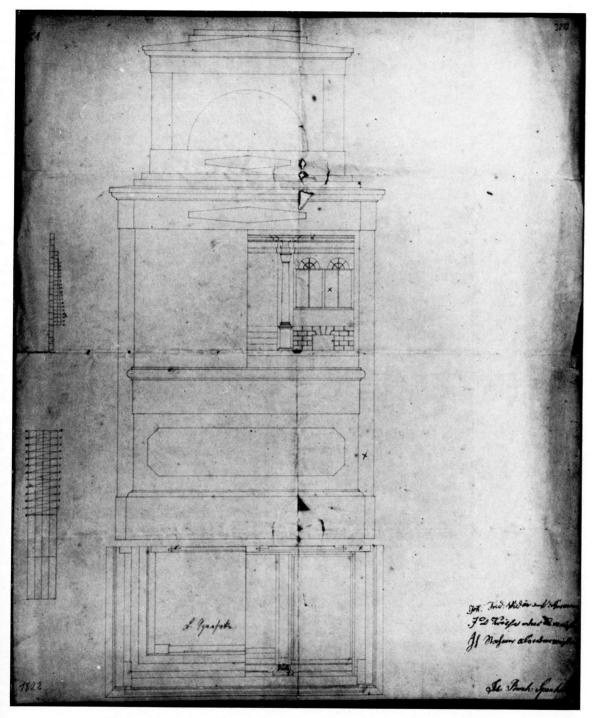

74. Masterpiece Design for a secretaire, by Bernhard Spanhake, Oldenburg, 1822
Landesmuseum für Kunst- und Kulturgeschichte, Oldenburg, inv. no. 3887/51. See p. 77

75. SOFA TABLE, Oldenburg, about 1825 to 1830
Veneered with mahogany, and inlaid with maple. H. 77, W. 141.5, D. 64
Landesmuseum für Kunst- und Kulturgeschichte, Oldenburg, inv. no. 1096. See p. 78

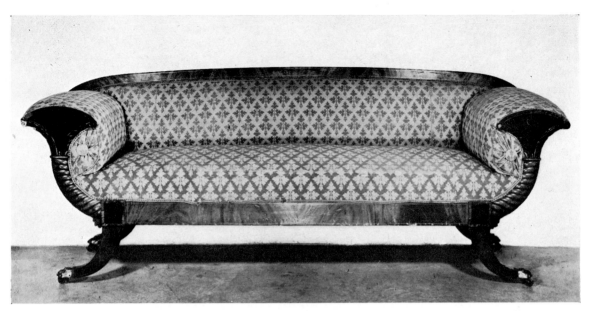

76. SOFA, Oldenburg, about 1820
Deal veneered with walnut. H. 85.5, W. 228, D. 67. Probably from the royal collection
Landesmuseum für Kunst- und Kulturgeschichte, Oldenburg, inv. no. 4069. See p. 78

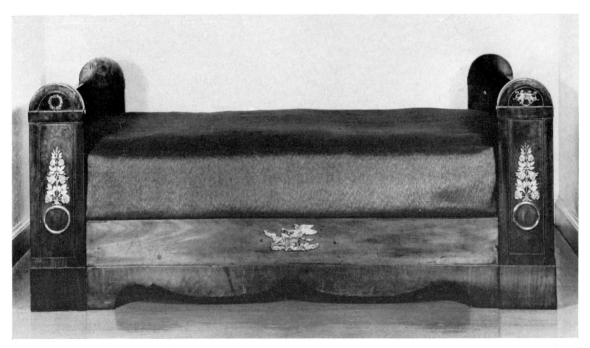

77. BED, Oldenburg, about 1815
Veneered with walnut, with bronze mounts. H. 78, L. 182, W. 91. Probably from the royal collection
Landesmuseum für Kunst- und Kulturgeschichte, Oldenburg, inv. no. 5357. See p. 78

78. SECRETAIRE, Schleswig-Holstein, about 1815 to 1820
Veneered with mahogany and stained walnut, with stamped mounts. On top of the fall front is a folding standing desk
H. 203, W. 108, D. 52.5
Museum für Kunst und Kulturgeschichte der Stadt Dortmund, Cappenberg. See p. 78

79. SECRETAIRE, Berlin, about 1815 to 1820
Veneered with mahogany, with bronze mounts. H. 190, W. 97, D. 50
Kunstgewerbemuseum, Berlin-Köpenick (Luthmer and Schmidt, plate 61a; Dammann, plate 17; Schmidt, plate 233;
Schade, plate 60). See p. 80

80. SECRETAIRE, Berlin, about 1825 to 1830. Designer: KARL FRIEDRICH SCHINKEL
Veneered with mahogany, with gilt bronze mounts. Once the property of Prince Wilhelm of Prussia
Formerly in the Dosquet Collection, Berlin (Schmitz, *Deutsche Möbel des Klassizismus*, plate 183;
Sievers, pp. 64ff, plate 142). See pp. 47, 80

81. DISPLAY CABINET, Berlin, about 1830. Designer: KARL FRIEDRICH SCHINKEL. Maker: KARL GEORG WANSCHAFF
Veneered with mahogany. H. 188.5, W. 115, D. 41
Verwaltung der Staatlichen Schlösser und Gärten, Berlin (Sievers, plate 149). See p. 81

82. SOFA, Berlin, about 1830. Designer: KARL FRIEDRICH SCHINKEL. Maker: KARL GEORG WANSCHAFF
Veneered with mahogany, and inlaid with maple. H. 90, W. 210.5, D. 77
Verwaltung der Staatlichen Schlösser und Gärten, Berlin (Sievers, plate 176). See p. 82

83. King Friedrich Wilhelm III's INVALID CHAIR, Berlin, about 1824. Designer: KARL FRIEDRICH SCHINKEL
Palisander, inlaid with hornbeam. H. 104, W. 94, D. 97
Schloss Charlottenburg, Berlin (Sievers, plate 114). See p. 82

84. SOFA, Berlin, about 1830
Veneered with mahogany. H. 101, W. 207, D. 71
Schloss Charlottenhof, Potsdam. See pp. 50, 82

85. CHAIR, Berlin, about 1820
Cherrywood. H. 84, W. 46, D. 41
Schloss Charlottenhof, Potsdam. See p. 82

86, 87. PATENT SECRETAIRE, Berlin, about 1815, by ADOLPH FRIEDRICH VOIGT
Veneered with ash root. H. 20, W. 64.5
Kunstgewerbemuseum, Berlin-Köpenick, inv. no. 24.37 (H. Schmitz, 'Ein Berliner Sekretär der Biedermeierzeit',
Berliner Museen, Berichte, XLVI, 1925, p. 35; Schade, plate 62). See pp. 42, 51, 83

88. COMMODE, Hanover, about 1820
Deal, veneered with mahogany, the interior of oak, with bronze mounts. H. 83.5, W. 101, D. 56
Herrenhausen Museum, Hanover. See p. 84

89. WORK TABLE, Hanover, about 1820 to 1825
Veneered with mahogany, and inlaid with maple, with a key-hole escutcheon of bone. H. 77, D. 42.7
Historisches Museum, Hanover, inv. no. VM 25165. See p. 84

90. GUILD CHEST, of the cobblers of Celle, 1830
Ash, with ebonized columns, and capitals of gilt stucco. H. 46, W. 67.5, D. 44
Bomann-Museum, Celle. See p. 84

91. SECRETAIRE, Hanover, about 1815

Veneered with mahogany and inlaid with maple, with gilt carved decoration, the upper feet green, those on the base of maple with incised leaf ornament, the top moulding of ebonized pearwood. H. 158, W. 93, D. 70

Kestner Museum, Hanover, inv. no. 4693 (Dammann, frontispiece; Luthmer and Schmidt, plate 112b; Feulner, 3rd ed., p. 745). See pp. 48, 84

92. SECRETAIRE, Rhineland, about 1820
Veneered with birch, with some mouldings ebonized. H. 182, W. 100, D. 49
Kunstsammlungen der Stadt, Düsseldorf, inv. no. 1956-8. A wardrobe en suite is in the same museum. See p. 85

93. TABLE, Rhineland, about 1825

Deal veneered with mahogany, the dolphins green and gold, the basket section ebonized. The top can be tilted. H. 79, D. 124

Museum für Kunst und Kulturgeschichte der Stadt Dortmund, Cappenberg, inv. no. C 3586. See p. 85

94. TABLE, Rhineland, about 1820 to 1825

Veneered with cherrywood, with gilt carved decoration. H. 76.5, D. 103.5

Bergisches Museum, Schloss Burg an der Wupper, inv. no. K/Mö 50 (J. C. Roselt, *Das Bergische Museum Schloss Burg an der Wupper*, Hamburg, 1969, p. 80). See pp. 50, 85

95. CHAIR, Rhineland, about 1820 to 1825
Veneered with cherrywood, with gilt carved
decoration. H. 89.5, W. 46.5
Bergisches Museum, Schloss Burg an der Wupper,
inv. no. K/Mö 51 (for references, see pl. 94). See p. 85

97. CHAIR, Rhineland–Westphalia, about 1825
Birch, with ebonized columns. H. 86, W. 45, D. 46
Museum für Kunst und Kulturgeschichte der Stadt
Dortmund, Cappenberg, inv. no. C 3253. See p. 85

96. SOFA, Rhineland, about 1825
Deal veneered with mahogany. H. 93.5, W. 200, D. 70
Museum für Kunst und Kulturgeschichte der Stadt Dortmund, Cappenberg. See p. 85

98. WORK TABLE, Rhineland-Westphalia, about 1820
Veneered with bird's-eye maple, with a walnut base, and ebonized legs. H. 80, D. 48.5
Museum für Kunst und Kulturgeschichte der Stadt Dortmund, Cappenberg, inv. no. C 3359

99. The composer Louis Spohr's Desk, Kassel, 1822
Veneered with cherrywood
Louis Spohr-Gedenk- und Forschungsstätte, Kassel (H. Homburg, *Louis Spohr*, Kassel, 1968, p. 111). See p. 86

100. SECRETAIRE, BERNHARD STEDEFELD'S masterpiece, Kassel, 1819
Veneered with walnut, the arched inset panel, and floral inlaid dome, together with the scallop motif and colonettes
in the interior veneered with ebonized maple and dark bird's-eye maple. H. 203, W. 106, D. 58.5
Universitätsmuseum, Marburg, inv. no. 2847 (The working drawing is also in the museum). (C. Graepler, *Marburger
Universitätsmuseum für Kunst und Kulturgeschichte, Auswahl aus den Sammlungen*, Marburg, 1964.) See p. 86

101. Secretaire by Hans Brandt, Thüringen, 1822
Deal veneered with mahogany, bird's-eye maple and birch, the rest of the interior of maple stained yellow
H. 200, W. 130, D. 50
Bomann-Museum, Celle. See p. 86

102. SECRETAIRE, LUDWIG BEISSNER's masterpiece, probably Thüringen, 1829
Deal veneered with mahogany, the interior façade of burr birch, oak and ebonized wood, the rest of the interior gaboon
H. 208.5, W. 124.5, D. 51.5
Museum für Kunst und Kulturgeschichte der Stadt Dortmund, Cappenberg, inv. no. C4474. See p. 86

103. SECRETAIRE, Thüringen, about 1815
Veneered with mahogany, the interior, veneered with birch, contains three gothic arched niches
with drawers behind them. H. 190, W. 94, D. 47
On the Munich art market. See p. 86

104. SECRETAIRE, LIENDE's masterpiece, probably Dresden, 1821
Pine and deal veneered with mahogany, the interior of oak. H. 187, W. 99.5, D. 49
Museum für Kunsthandwerk, Dresden, inv. no. 39451 (G. Messner, 'Zu einigen Möbelneuerwerbungen des Museums
für Kunsthandwerk, Dresden', *Staatliche Kunstsammlungen Dresden, Jahrbuch 1967*, p. 143). See p. 86

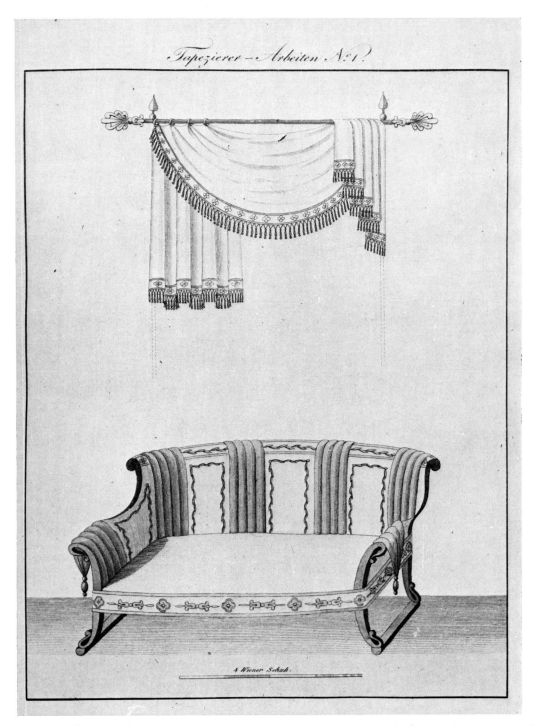

105. Drapery and 'geschweiftes Canapé, nach der neuesten Art gearbeitet und verziret' (curved SOFA, executed and decorated in the most modern manner), by the middle-class upholsterer and decorator, LECHNER of Vienna

From W. C. W. Blumenbach, *Wiener Kunst- und Gewerbsfreund oder der neueste Wiener Geschmack*, Vienna, 1825. See pp. 88, 89

106. DESIGN for a chair by JOSEF DANHAUSER, Vienna, about 1820
Watercolour
Österreichisches Museum für angewandte Kunst, Vienna, sheet 8971/64. See p. 89

107. JOHANN HEINRICH KRUPPEL, the younger. *View of the Green Salon in the Bürglass-Schlösschen in Coburg* (detail)
1832. Pen and watercolour. 33.8 × 57.3
Kunstsammlungen der Veste Coburg, inv. no. 4076. See p. 89

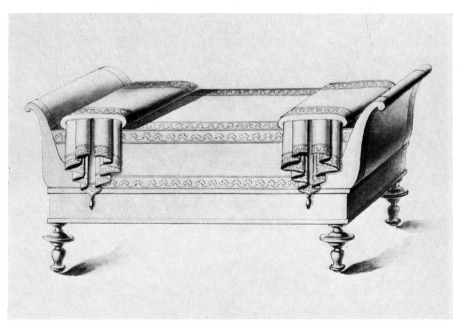

108. DESIGN for a bed with 'Couvertrahmen' (framed coverlet) by JOSEF DANHAUSER, Vienna, about 1825
Pen and watercolour
Österreichisches Museum für angewandte Kunst, Vienna, sheet XVIII/332. See p. 89

109. KING FERDINAND V OF HUNGARY'S SECRETAIRE, Vienna, about 1830 to 1835
H. 162, W. 89.5, D. 42

Städtisches Museum, Prague (J. Durdik and others, *Das grosse Bilderlexikon der Antiquitäten*, Prague, 1968, Plate 53)

See p. 96

110. Desk by A. Einholzer, Vienna, 1836
Cherrywood. H. 105, W. 133, D. 80
Kunstauktion des Dorotheum, Vienna, sale number 579 (19/22.iii.1968), lot 974
A design with some variations is *Österreichisches Museum für angewandte Kunst, Vienna, Sheet XVIII g 88*, p. 8
A similar piece is illustrated in Lux, plate 30. See p. 97

111. Work Table, North Germany, about 1830 to 1835
Ebonized beech and pearwood, with stamped mounts. H. 80, W. 70.5, D. 44.5
Landesmuseum für Kunst- und Kulturgeschichte, Oldenburg, inv. no. 7107. See p. 97

112. SOFA, Berlin, about 1830 to 1835
H. 95, W. 202, D. 75
Schloss Charlottenhof, Potsdam. See pp. 51, 97

113. SOFA, Munich, about 1830 to 1835
Deal veneered with walnut, the applied leaf decoration was originally ebonized. H. 111, W. 216, D. 68.5
Schlossmuseum, Berchtesgaden. See p. 97

114. Four CHAIRS, Prague, about 1830 to 1835
H. 90, W. 43, D. 43
Národni Galerie, Prague (J. Durdik and others, *Das grosse Bilderlexikon der Antiquitäten*, Prague, 1968, plate 55)
See p. 97

115. ARMCHAIR by MICHAEL THONET, Boppard am Rhein, about 1836
Walnut, constructed of thin strips glued together and bent. H. 88.5, W. 53, D. 53
Bayerisches Nationalmuseum, Munich, inv. no. 69/2. See p. 98

Index